An Engineer's Guide to the

SPIRIT WORLD

My Journey from Skeptic
to Psychic Medium

*For my friend Peri —
to remind you that
reality is stranger than
we can imagine*

JOHN RONCZ

john roncz

Contact the author:
www.johnroncz.com

ISBN 13: 978-1478221944
ISBN 10: 1478221941

Cover Photo: NASA, ESA, T. Megeath, M. Robberto
Interior Photos: John Roncz
Hebrew and Christian Bible Quotations: Translated from
Hebrew and Greek sources by John Roncz
Book Editing and Design: Kenneth Guentert.
The Publishing Pro, LLC, Colorado Springs, Colorado

Contents

Preface

WRITING THIS BOOK is something I felt compelled to do. Yet it is also a frightening thing to do. I feel like I'm about to appear on television in front of a vast audience, naked. My career in aviation has made me a minor hero to the people involved in the world of airplanes and has brought me many honors. I have a wall full of them. If you're interested, I've written an appendix about my work as a specialist in a branch of aeronautical engineering called aerodynamics. But this book is not about airplanes.

Not that many years ago I put the people who believed in an afterlife, spirits, or things that violated the observable laws of nature in the same category as those who believed in Santa Claus and the Easter Bunny. If it could not be observed and measured, for me it was not worth thinking about.

There is an old saying that if you want to get a mule's attention, first you hit it in the head with a two-by-four. Well, I got whacked in a temple in Egypt, and my whole belief system was rattled by it. The things that started happening to me afterward were so preposterous that in telling my story I wondered whether anyone would believe it. Yet every word is true.

The big question, of course, is the one Moses asked: Why me? I've thought about that a lot. The only answer I can give is that my distinguished reputation as an engineer gives me a level of credibility that perhaps other people doing this work do not have. I've spent more than thirty years using the laws of physics to work on some amazing airplanes. I've lectured all over the country on that subject. I am nobody's fool, and it took a lot to convince me that the spirit world is real. While I may be an expert in the laws governing flight, I came to admit that I know almost nothing about how the universe really works. Actually, nobody knows how the universe works. All the matter and energy that can be sensed or measured is only 4.8 percent of what's really there. The rest is called Dark Energy and Dark Matter. Nobody knows what these are.

That's what intrigues me the most. I want to understand how this invisible world works. I can't help it; I'm still an engineer. So while I'm communicating with someone who no longer has a physical body, I'm analyzing how I'm getting the information. With every reading I learn more about the spirit world. In this book I share what I've learned.

Thanks for joining me on this search for answers.

John Roncz

Acknowledgments

FIRST, I WANT TO THANK John Holland, whose reading first convinced me that getting information from deceased friends was possible. Thanks also to Pat McKenna and Glenn Klausner, who pushed me much further down the path with their readings.

The education I've received at the Arthur Findlay College has vastly improved my confidence and my skills. I'm so grateful for the opportunity to have worked with some outstanding mediums and teachers there: Sue Taylor, Glyn Edwards, Mavis Pitilla, Simon James, Simone Key, Brenda Lawrence, Kitty Woud, Eamonn Downey, and Colin Bates. Their dedication to serving as voices for the spirit world is contagious. Thanks also to Scott Milligan and David Thompson for showing us what physical mediumship is capable of doing. I look forward to my next course at the college with enthusiasm.

I also want to thank Joyce Hug, who has encouraged me to work publicly at Sacred Waters. Joyce also went through the manuscript with a fine-toothed comb and made many comments and suggestions that were very helpful. Thanks also to Roger Lanphear for reviewing Chapter Ten, and to Professor Peri Arnold for his comments on that chapter.

Finally, I cannot say enough good things about Kenneth Guentert and The Publishing Pro. His dedication to making this a readable book was obvious at every stage. I feel very fortunate to have him as my editor.

BOOK ONE
*How the Spirit World
Got My Attention*

Chapter 1

My Trip to Egypt

I USED TO WATCH a television program called *Sightings* every day while eating lunch. I had always been interested in subjects like UFOs. I figured there had to be something to UFOs, because too many trained civilian and military pilots had reported encounters with them. In World War II, our fighter planes and bombers often encountered bright balls of light, which they named "Foo Fighters."

One particular day the subject of *Sightings* was "medical intuition." The program interviewed doctors who described how they occasionally encountered a patient who had obvious symptoms, but their tests were unable to pinpoint the cause. In these cases, the doctors phoned medical intuitive Caroline Myss, who had this amazing ability to identify the underlying cause just by learning the name of the person and the date of his or her birth. For example, sometimes the illness was caused by a tumor hiding in a place that X rays would miss. I was intrigued. How could that be possible? Toward the end of the program they interviewed her. She described how everything is made up of energy and explained that she could perceive an image of where in the body that energy was leaking and, from that, which organ was in distress. Her description of the universe as a web of energy matched the mental picture that I had developed over many years studying physics.

After the program ended, I went to my computer and searched for Caroline's website. On the very first page was an invitation: "Come with me to Egypt." I looked at this and instantly said, "Okay." She was going to be the featured speaker on a tour organized by Power Places Tours.

Egypt had always fascinated me. The size, scope, and age of their monuments were staggering, especially considering that they constructed these monuments without modern tools. I called my long-suffering friend Tim and asked, "Wanna go to Egypt?"

He said, "Okay, I'll go." Tim was a good friend. His career as a real estate developer gave him the freedom to take time off and the resources to do so. He was always open to another crazy adventure with me, and he shared my interest in Egyptian history.

The Great Pyramid

So, in early 1999, the two of us flew to Cairo and joined the group, which was staying at the Mena House Hotel in the shadow of the pyramids. We spent part of the day as tourists with private guides and part of the day listening to Caroline's lectures. For the tours, we were divided into groups. Our group leader was a Dr. Fathi, who had been employed by the Cairo Museum in charge of the treasures of Tutankhamun. Dr. Fathi is highly respected and knowledgeable, and we were lucky to have him. The tour leaders made special arrangements for us to visit the best sites while they were closed to the public.

One of the perks of our private tour was an opportunity to enter the Great Pyramid of Khufu at Giza late at night, even though it was closed to the public. Our small group of five climbed up the large casing stones to a hole in the side about 50 feet above the ground and went inside. Facing us was a small passage, 3½-feet wide and less than 4-feet high, angling up at a steep 26-degree angle for 129 feet. Because of the small size of the tunnel, we were forced to bend at the waist and climb the steep floor hunched over. I was nervous, because if anyone ahead of us lost their footing, the unfortunate person would slide back down—and all of us would go tumbling to the bottom. Fortunately, this did not happen. When we finally reached the top, we could stand upright again. My legs throbbed with pain. We were now inside what they call the grand gallery. It is about 7-feet wide and 28-feet high—and rises at the same 26-degree angle for 157 feet. It is one of the most amazing things I've ever seen. It was like entering a cathedral in the midst of a mountain. At the top of this passage is a room, which is situated about fourteen stories above the ground and had once been sealed off with huge granite doors. The whole room is made of pink granite, the hardest material in Egypt. It had been brought down the Nile from Aswan, about 600 miles away. There is an unfinished granite box in this room, which may have been designed as a sarcophagus for the pharaoh Khufu. Its unfinished state, and the lack of a lid anywhere for it, suggests that it was never used. We sat down and began some simple chanting, listening to the echoes reverberating off the ancient walls. After most of the other people left, I decided to lie down inside the granite box to see if I'd feel anything. We arranged to have the lights turned off at a specific time because I wanted to do a time exposure with my camera to see if it could pick up light or other images. Tim left because he didn't want to stay inside the pyramid in total darkness.

I tried an experiment with sound while still lying inside the granite box. I sang a constant tone, slowly sliding up and down the scale. When I got to a particular frequency, the whole box vibrated, banging my head against the bottom and amplifying the sound. I tried this several times with the same result. Apparently the box is tuned to a particular note, although I cannot imagine why.

Facing My Fear

I was the last person to leave. It was late at night as I walked down from the Giza plateau towards the Mena House. The only street is narrow and dark, and I was walking down the center of it, looking very touristy with my camera hanging around my neck. About a block ahead of me I saw a tall Arab man, mean-looking, standing in the middle of the street with his arms folded across his chest. He was staring at me. The street was otherwise empty. My heart pounded. There was no other route; no way around this man. Surely I was going to be robbed or killed.

I remembered one of the lectures we had with Caroline. She taught us that thoughts are energy and that, if we spend that energy being afraid, all that negativity will pile up and bring about the very thing we are afraid of. That registered with me. I recall that my cousin Rose was terrified of getting cancer. If she read an article claiming that some substance might cause cancer, she would eliminate it from her life. As you might have guessed, Rose died from cancer. All the energy she put into that fear brought about the very thing she was afraid of.

Lacking any other alternative, I kept walking down the street. I tried to reign in my fear and think of a positive reason for this man blocking the road. I came up with the theory that he was there to protect me, and I tried my best to convince myself of this. But if this were true, what should I do? I decided that I should thank him. So I walked right up to him in the middle of the street, looked up at him, and said, "Thank you." He looked down at me and said in a thick accent, "You are very welcome, Sir, and welcome to Egypt." It was a profound lesson for me, one that I will never forget.

We spent a few more days in Cairo, going out to visit three other pyramids. We also spent an entire afternoon at the incredible Cairo Museum. It was an amazing experience to look upon the face of Ramesses II and to walk around the gold mask of Tutankhamun studying the details. I left with a profound sense of awe at what the Egyptian civilization had produced.

I found the Egyptian people to be friendly and very honest. I have to admit that it took me a while to adjust to the culture. For example, Tim and I visited a shop that made and sold drawings on papyrus. I tried my hand at making paper from the papyrus plants, and soon the shopkeepers had us sitting down, drinking hot sweet tea, and smoking the hookah. Doing business is a social occasion in Egypt, and I had to fight my normal impatience at first. But once I got used to it, it was a wonderful thing. I gained much respect for the values that their Muslim religion has taught them. Our bus driver would sometimes sing passages from the Quran to pass the time. Five times a day the call to prayer resonated across the city from the minarets of all the mosques. I found it very soothing and comforting.

The Temple of Karnak

The tour continued with a flight to the city of Luxor. In ancient times it was called Thebes. There are two famous temples there: the Temple of Luxor and the Temple of Karnak. Across from Thebes is the famous Valley of the Kings, where many pharaohs were buried, including Tutankhamun. We stayed at the Sonesta hotel in the center of the city of Luxor.

One morning, we got up very early to visit the Karnak temple before it was open to the public. Dr. Fathi walked us through this amazing complex—the largest in Egypt. It covers 247 acres, and was continuously enlarged over 1,300 years. I don't think anything can prepare you for the majesty of this place. I felt like a dwarf among the 82-foot tall columns in the hypostyle hall. In the time that we had, Dr. Fathi could only show us a few of the major features, including the holy place where the statue of Amun was placed. As an engineer, I tried to imagine how they built all these things. The effort involved had to be staggering. I could have spent a month there and still not have seen everything.

After Dr Fathi finished our brief tour, he told us that we were free to explore the temple, as long as we were back at the bus in an hour. I wanted to take some photos, so I went off on my own, walking around a lake and through some rubble, searching for good camera shots. I was fairly far from where I started when I came upon a smaller temple with four statues outside. I went inside and, because there were no interior lights, I waited for my eyes to adjust to the dark. Eventually, I saw that at the end of the corridor were two doors, one going left and one going right. I walked down the center hall and entered the doorway to the right. It was even darker inside, so I stood still. Suddenly I felt shaking, and my immediate reaction was that we were having a mild earthquake. But the shaking didn't stop. Then I smelled incense—a sweet wooden scent. I wondered who had come here to burn incense. The shaking and the incense continued. At first I thought, "This is cool!" But as it continued, I thought to myself, "This is getting scary." I wished that Tim were there. Within a millisecond of that thought, Tim appeared in the doorway, which was even more startling. In a remote area of a 247-acre complex, how could he magically appear at the exact instant that I wanted him there?

The shaking stopped, but the incense smell lingered. I asked Tim if he could smell the incense. He replied that he couldn't smell anything because his sinuses were all plugged up. As we left the temple I told him exactly what had happened. We made our way back to the bus, where Dr. Fathi was waiting for us. I wanted to know where I had been, so I drew a map in the sand. He told me that this was the temple of Khonsu, who was the son of Amun and Mut, the chief god and goddess. "That's an interesting place," he added. When I pressed him for more information, he explained that there was a legend associated with that temple.

The legend claimed that from time to time Khonsu would see someone in the temple complex that he loves and call that person to himself—always alone, never with anyone else—and bless him with incense. I had goose bumps the size of camels. Tim had to tell him what had happened to me because I was speechless. That night Dr Fathi took me to a jeweler friend of his, who made a special symbol on a gold chain for me, saying that it is a symbol of divine protection.

This was my first supernatural encounter. I know what I experienced, and I could not find any way of rationalizing it; it was what it was. Why me? How could Tim be drawn to the same place, only to appear at the exact instant that I wanted him there? It left me with many unanswered questions.

A Marked Man?

This was not to be the end of the story. Later that year, I was looking for another adventure and found a reasonably priced cruise from Athens to Cape Town over a five-week period. I called Tim. "Wanna go to Africa?"

He replied, "Okay, I'll go."

We sailed from Athens through the Suez Canal and docked in Safaga. From there we took a bus to Luxor and stayed for a couple of days. This time our hotel was outside of town by a few miles, so we had to take a taxi. We came out of the hotel to see a line of taxis waiting. But one taxi cut in front of the others, getting murderous looks from the other taxi drivers. Its driver opened the door and politely invited us in.

I really didn't care which taxi we took. The surprise was that this driver would not leave us. Tim loves to shop, and it was really convenient that however long we were away, our taxi would still be there waiting for us. The driver endured threats and curses from the other drivers because they were supposed to take turns. But for us it was great to be able to leave things in the taxi as we explored the many shops.

We also visited the hotel we had stayed at on our tour with

Power Places, and the staff came out from behind the desk with huge grins saying, "John, you're back!" They remembered us. Even the street vendor outside greeted us like long lost brothers. It felt wonderful to be back there.

At the end of a long day it was time to return to the hotel. Tim gathered up all his purchases and headed for the room. I wondered how much this full day of taxi service was going to cost us. I figured we owed this man $50–$60, but it was worth it for the incredible service. I asked him how much I owed him. He said that he could not take any money from me. Whoa! What kind of scam is this? He just kept repeating that it was an honor for him to have me in his taxi and that he didn't want anything from me. He kept repeating this with tears in his eyes, and I finally realized that he was serious. I gave him a one dollar bill, pointing out the pyramid on the back. He held it up in front of him saying that he would always keep it and that he would always remember me.

Once again, I was stunned. What was that all about?

Several months later, I had to phone a man about some engineering work and spent quite a while on the phone with his secretary. I mentioned that I had been in Egypt. As it turned out, she and her husband had spent a long time there. I told her about my experience with the taxi.

She said simply, "You are marked somehow, and some Egyptians can see the mark." I had not said anything about my experience at the temple of Khonsu. But as crazy as it sounded, it was the first explanation that made some kind of sense to me. What was this mark? What did it mean?

It was not the last experience of this kind. A few years later I was staying on the island of Kauai. I had reserved the cheapest economy car and, after getting my paperwork, I went over to the row where they were parked. The lady who was in the little booth where you stopped before exiting walked over to me, gave me a big smile, and told me that I could take any car I wanted. I walked past the compact cars, and the midsize cars, finally choosing a full size Chevy. I was really surprised and pleased. I hoped that she wouldn't get in trouble for that.

After checking into my hotel and changing into normal Hawaiian clothes, I went shopping for groceries at Safeway. At the checkout lane, there were three carts ahead of me and two behind me. We all had full carts. A middle-aged man came over to me, and signaled me to follow him. He unhooked the chain on a far checkout lane, and after I had pushed my cart into the lane, he reconnected the chain. He rang up my groceries, then called to another man to ask for some kind of code. He entered the code into the cash register, and my bill was reduced by 20 percent. As I was paying the bill, he looked at me and said, "People like us have to stick together."

I had no explanation for this, but it was another example of being singled out for special treatment. Kauai is a very spiritual place, and I wondered if he had somehow seen Khonsu's invisible mark.

The Voices of Childhood

I had never considered myself anything special. In fact, I had grown up feeling exactly the opposite.

My father was a skilled athlete, born to Hungarian immigrants who settled in the small rural town of Divernon, Illinois. He was a gregarious person who made friends easily and seldom forgot the name of anyone he met. When Japan attacked Pearl Harbor, he quit college and went to enlist in the Army Air Corps. He saw active duty in Europe as a bombardier, and although he didn't talk about the war very much, he did tell me that dropping bombs on Hungary really bothered him. He earned the Distinguished Flying Cross for saving the life of a crewmate by holding the severed ends of an artery together while the bomber flew home in the bitter high altitude cold.

Dad had wanted to play professional baseball. He played in the minor leagues and was offered a position with the Cincinnati Reds. That goal was cut short when he had an auto accident on the way to training. I was their first child and, as it turned out, the only boy. When I was born, he ran around bragging that I had the big hands of a baseball player.

I was a terrible disappointment to my father. He wanted to teach his son all those things that he found so important and enjoyable in his life. He tried to play ball with me. I could not catch or hit a ball, and I had no interest in doing so. He tried taking me hunting. I did manage to shoot a rabbit once, and I still carry the guilt from murdering that little bunny. Dad also liked planting and working in a garden in our back yard. I had no particular desire to play in the dirt.

I failed miserably to enjoy all those things that carried enormous importance to Dad. I never even expressed a desire to learn about them. The end result was that Dad played with the other neighborhood boys, praising their athletic skills at dinner time. I did not fit his vision of what I should be, and he didn't hide his disappointment.

Two years after my own debut, my sister Diane was born. She was the jock Dad had always wanted. She would run around with my cowboy guns shooting up the neighborhood while I stayed indoors and cooked little cakes in her Easy-Bake Oven. In a way I was off the hook. Diane would go with Dad to ball games, while I was left alone.

Four years after Diane came Maribeth. Within a year Mom was pregnant again. While they were expecting their fourth child, we moved to a new house—a ranch house finished with Indiana limestone. It was a step up from the cracker box that was their starter home. Then my third sister, Janet, was born.

My status in this foursome was pretty clear. The house had three bedrooms. Mom and Dad shared the big room at the end of the hall. The middle bedroom belonged to Diane alone, but I shared the smallest room with my two baby sisters. In retrospect this was a strange arrangement. Later in life I brought this up to Diane. I was the oldest and the only boy, so why those sleeping arrangements? Diane thought about it for a moment and said, "That *was* weird!"

While I was in seventh grade my parents purchased a new, two-story home. I'll never forget the first time we kids went to see it. The bedrooms were upstairs. The large room at the end of the hallway went to my sister Diane. Its centerpiece was a huge poster bed, so high up that there was a little upholstered staircase to climb up into it. She had two dressers and a large closet. Next to it was the master bedroom, which seemed huge to my eyes. Near the top of the stairs was a third, smaller room that had two beds for my two youngest sisters. I remember feeling almost sick when I realized there were no more rooms and no more beds.

On the main floor was the kitchen with a breakfast nook, a formal dining room, and a living room, with a spinet piano against the wall. Flanking the fireplace were two couches, which we were never allowed to sit on. Finally, there was a small room, which held the family television, one couch, a small roll-top desk that mom used to pay bills, and a collapsible table against the opposite wall. Next to the television was an old decorated milk can that held umbrellas. Next to the couch was an antique stove that was being used as a lamp stand. This, I was told, would be my room. I still can't remember where my clothes were. There was one closet in the room, but it contained heavy winter coats and raincoats for the whole family. I slept on the couch.

The worst part of not having a room was the lack of a place to do my homework or do anything else requiring space. At nighttime, I could not go to sleep until Dad stopped watching the television, so I often didn't get to sleep until late, and then had trouble getting up in the morning. Because there were six of us and only one couch, most of the time I spread out on the floor with my books to do my homework.

From first to eighth grade, I attended Saint Joseph's Catholic Grade School. Most classes were taught by nuns. I liked school. I was good at learning, never caused trouble, and soon became the teacher's pet. The attention I got at school was a big contrast to the feelings of inadequacy and disappointment that I felt from Dad.

Years later I presented him with a college report card showing straight A's. It was a feeble attempt to get some kind of praise from him. He looked it over, then shot me down. "What are you studying that shit for?" he said in a tone that combined both annoyance and contempt. Obviously, I was a complete waste of money.

I grew up feeling that there was something terribly wrong with me, that in some way I was defective. I never tried to make friends with the neighborhood boys and was shy around people my age. This would haunt me well into later life.

So the idea that in some way I was special was totally foreign to me. I just didn't understand it.

Chapter 2

How the Spirit World Recruited Me

FROM THE TIME I experienced my first supernatural experience at the temple of Karnak in 1999, I began to do some serious research. For example, I read books on the paranormal. Tim gave me a book on mysticism. I learned that mystics seemed to have similar experiences regardless of which religion they belonged to.

I also began to study Kabbalah, which is the mystical branch of Judaism. I had always thought that if people were truly in touch with divine knowledge, then they should be able to tell me things that nobody on earth knew. It struck me that the Kabbalists understood that the universe came from a single point, exploding into existence. Today we call that the Big Bang. How could they know that?

I have always been interested in physics because I like to know how things work. As a child I would get in trouble for taking things apart—and not being able to put them back together again. For example, my mother was not happy to find her cuckoo clock in pieces. I've also tried to understand superstring theory. The concept is that all matter is made up of very tiny strings vibrating in ten dimensions of space, forming all the subatomic particles we know of. I looked at the ten symbols on the Kabbalist's Tree of Life and wondered if this was just a coincidence.

I had encountered something very unusual in Egypt, something that had apparently left its mark on me, and I needed to know more. As a result my horizon widened to include all kinds of esoteric knowledge.

A Psychic Cruise with My Mother

When I was growing up, my mother told me the story of how she had almost drowned in a boating accident that took the life of her younger sister. Mom said that she had glimpsed another world. After that, she became very religious—and attracted to psychics. When she heard of a new psychic, she would drive for hours to listen to him or her. When the top of our refrigerator became covered with cassette tapes of psychic readings, we began to think she was pretty crazy. At a minimum, I thought that she was wasting a lot of time and money. But it was her life, and if it made her feel better, then I was okay with it

After Dad retired, my parents bought a house in Lehigh Acres, a small town near Fort Myers, Florida. Their house sat on a golf course, which was notable because golfers occasionally would be chased by alligators. A few months after Dad retired, he suffered a severe heart attack. He hung on for a few years, but he had to take life more slowly because he no longer had his usual stamina. Finally, he suffered kidney failure, was unable to tolerate dialysis, and passed away.

After Dad died, I made it a point to fly to Florida at least once a year to spend time with Mom. I had gone on cruises with my parents, and Mom really enjoyed them. I decided I should continue the tradition. I would find web sites that offered amazing last-minute prices on cruises leaving out of Miami or Fort Lauderdale, and I would book a three- or four-day cruise. Then Mom and I would drive to the port to board our ship, traversing the famous Alligator Alley that bisects the Everglades. Depending on the time of year, the highway could be covered with snakes or frogs. I hated the crunching sounds under the wheels, but there was no way to avoid hitting them.

Sharing a cabin and our meals away from normal distractions was a good way for us to spend time together. We both enjoyed playing the slot machines, and we liked to play Bingo every day. Sometimes one of us would win something. Mom really enjoyed these cruises, so it became an annual tradition.

Because of her interest in psychics, a cruise in April 2001 caught my eye. It was sponsored by the Intuitive Vision Network and featured some lectures by psychics and mediums. I knew that she would really enjoy this one. I booked the cruise and, in addition, signed up the two of us for a group sitting with medium Suzane Northrop. I didn't know what to expect, but Mom was excited by the prospect. I also booked a private session with John Holland, and this would change my life forever.

When the cruise ship was at sea, Mom and I went to one of the conference rooms and listened to talks on a variety of subjects. Most of what I heard did not register with me at all because it did not match my own experiences. Maybe Archangel Michael really is available for house calls, but I wasn't buying it. Others spoke about their spirit guides who would advise them on every decision. I had never met a spirit guide, so I remained skeptical. I was going to need a lot more evidence before I could believe these things.

Of course, you could say the same thing about physics. Physicists still do not know why anything has mass. If particles did not have mass, there would be no gravity and nothing would clump together. Goodbye, Universe. Dig inside the components of an atom, and you'll find that they are made of something smaller called quarks. They come in sets of three. Yet a quark does not have a diameter. How can something that has no dimension exist? Then there is the whole idea of the universe having ten dimensions of space, of which we can only experience three: length, width and height. Reality truly is stranger than fiction.

Then it was time for Mom and me to go to the cabin for a group sitting with Suzane. It was rather strange. Suzane entered into what she called a "trance state." She paced barefoot around the room while speaking loudly in a strange, unidentifiable foreign accent. She did tell Mom and me that she had a link with my sister Diane, who had passed away from liver cancer. She told us that Diane was working with seeing-eye dogs, helping the dogs to lead their blind masters. Diane loved dogs, and I could truly imagine her doing this. She also picked up on my best friend Alan, who had dropped dead from a heart attack in the shower at the age of thirty-eight. The information was accurate, although her style seemed rather strange to me. But then I had never been to anything like this before. There was no way to prove that Diane was working with dogs. But there was enough evidence, both for us and for other people in the group, to prove that she was getting information somehow that she had no rational way of knowing.

When the time came for my private meeting with John Holland, I went to his cabin. John sat on his bed and I sat in his chair. It was just a conversation. No trance, no unusual accent. It was a much more comfortable environment for me. John picked up on my father right away. He also said that I had three friends who had died young. One of them was Alan. John told me that someone in that family had experienced car problems. I didn't know about that. He also talked about some kind of religious object that had been handed down in his family. I didn't know about that either. He told me that Alan had four children, and the oldest looked just like him. That was true. He also said that one of his sons wanted to move further away from his mother and that his mother was not happy about that. John told me to tell her that "Dad" (Alan) said it was okay, that she should let him go. The other person he brought through was a high-school classmate of mine. Mike had committed suicide. John correctly identified some specific information about him. He also explained some of the issues that had caused his severe depression. Although the session ended before he could bring up the third friend, I knew who it was. Jim had died in a plane crash.

When I got home, I called Alan's widow, Judy. She had the car trouble. She didn't know what this object was that had been passed down in the family. Her youngest son wanted to enlist in the army, and she was opposed to that. So I passed on that her late husband advised her to let him go. Later I spoke to her oldest son. He had visited his mother, and while looking through a closet, he found a silver cup that belonged to his great-grandfather. The cup is used for making a blessing over wine on the Jewish Sabbath. He took the cup home and polished it up. So John was right about the object that had been handed down.

The private sitting with John convinced me that some people could actually get information from someone who had died. Furthermore, my dead friend Alan also proved that he is still aware of what's going on in his family. That's an utterly amazing thought. If our consciousness and memories survive beyond our physical bodies, it's the most important piece of information we could ever have. This could not have been a case of John reading my mind, although that alone would have been impressive. I had no knowledge of the car trouble, the cup, or that Judy's youngest child wanted to join the army. How could John be reading my mind if I didn't even know about those things? That information had to be coming from my dead friend Alan. I was skeptical, but John had proven to me that this was a real phenomenon, with staggering implications.

I played the tape recording of that session for my mother on the drive back to Fort Myers. She confirmed some of the information that my father had told John. Mom had always believed in an afterlife, so it was not as shocking to her as it was to me. Then I flew home to Indiana.

Chocolate Chips, Sushi, and Slot Machines

My usual morning routine is to go to the kitchen immediately after waking up. I open the cabinet door, take out a coffee filter, and put it in the coffee machine. I put in the coffee, fill the water reservoir, and start the coffee brewing. Then I go take a shower, and when I'm done my coffee is ready.

One morning I opened the cabinet door, and in front of the box of coffee filters was half a bag of chocolate chips. The bag was folded in half, and the top was sealed with a wide yellow clip. I stared at this and started laughing. I have never bought a bag of chocolate chips in my life, nor did I own a yellow clip. "So I don't get a whole bag?" I asked. I thought it was hilarious. If the Universe decided to materialize chocolate chips, why not a whole bag? This was to be the first of many such experiences.

My friend Sean is a massage therapist. He's a bit taller than me, with bright blue eyes that sparkle with his wonderful sense of humor. Sean had gone through a lot in his life and had developed a great interest in spirituality. Among other things, he taught me to see the auras, which are little energy clouds, surrounding trees.

Sean and I both like sushi. Fortunately, there is a good sushi restaurant about twelve miles away. One week, we talked about meeting on Friday night at the sushi restaurant. At that time Sean ran his own massage therapy business, and his schedule was erratic. We agreed to touch base late on Friday afternoon and, if he was free, to meet later at the restaurant.

All week long I looked forward to having sushi with Sean. Finally Friday came, and I gave him a call around six P.M. to set a time to meet. Unfortunately, he was busy that evening. I was really disappointed. I hung up the phone, and at precisely the same instant the doorbell rang. It confused me for a moment, because the timing was so perfect it seemed as if hanging up the phone had somehow rung the doorbell.

I went to the front door. Standing there was a boy, about twelve or thirteen years old. He had blue eyes and a blond crew cut—and he was holding a platter of sushi! He said simply, "I heard you like sushi, so I brought you some."

I was utterly speechless. My house sits a good distance from the street and is isolated. Nobody in Elkhart, Indiana, goes door to door with sushi! I tried to thank him, but I was so stunned that I could only fumble for words. I took the sushi the short distance to the kitchen, removed the plastic wrap, and sniffed. It smelled fresh and wonderful. There was a small pile of wasabi, but no soy sauce. I set it down on the kitchen island, and reached to open the refrigerator. Touching the refrigerator door rang the doorbell. Once again it startled me. I walked over to the front door and opened it. Here was the same boy, holding a small plastic bag with about a quarter cup of soy sauce in it. "I'm sorry, I forgot the soy sauce," he said, holding the little bag out at arm's length. I couldn't believe this. Once again I mumbled some kind of thanks and closed the door.

As I was eating the excellent sushi, it occurred to me that this boy could not have walked to the end of the driveway in the time it took me to set the platter down and reach for the refrigerator. There was no car in the drive, so obviously he walked. I had never seen him before, nor have I seen him since. The only sushi restaurant does not deliver; and if they did, it would not be via a young boy.

I had another strange experience involving Sean. He had a bad toothache and needed a root canal and a crown. This was going to cost $1,500, which he did not have. I wished I had the money. I would rather have given it to him than see him in pain.

The next morning I woke up, fired up the computer, checked the weather and my email. For some reason I decided to check the boarding times for a casino boat in Michigan City, Indiana. At that time, Indiana law permitted casinos, but they had to be classified as river boats. The casinos were large barges that were able to move on the water—at least theoretically. To complete the fiction, the casinos published "boarding times," even though they never moved an inch.

I didn't like this particular casino, but I had gone there a couple of times with friends. I could not get the idea of going there out of my head, as much as I tried to dismiss it. I ended up in the car driving an hour away to Michigan City with $28 in my wallet. When I arrived there, I found a big circus tent in the parking lot. There was some kind of special event going on, and the place was packed. I finally went inside, and there were so many people it was hard to make my way into the boat. With $28 I thought I would play a nickel machine, but I couldn't even get into the room. I went upstairs, and it was packed also. I went downstairs and finally found a dollar machine that was open. I didn't want to play dollars, so I wandered around for a while, but that one machine was the only one that wasn't being played.

I decided to put in $20, lose the $20, get this out of my system, and then go home. The machine was called a "Double Double Diamond" machine. Although you could play $2 at a time, I had only $20 and decided to play single dollars. Within a couple of minutes, I was down to $8. Then I heard a voice in my head say, "play two coins." I decided that it didn't matter because I was going to lose anyway. I hit the "maximum bet" button. The reels spun around and landed on three "double diamond" symbols. I sat there in shock. I had just won the maximum jackpot of $4,000! I thought about Khonsu, chocolate chips, and sushi, and marveled at how the Universe had just pulled off another miracle.

The machine was making a lot of noise to attract people to the fact that sometimes jackpots are actually won. Eventually, someone came and took my driver's license, because the IRS wanted their cut, and they took their sweet time coming back with a W2G tax form and forty $100 bills. It was unreal.

Later that week, I invited Sean over for dinner. I put a salad bowl in front of him with fifteen $100 bills in it.

"I can't take your money, John."

"Believe me, the money is not from me. Besides, I have twenty-five more of those bills over there." Then I told him the story. Sean got his tooth fixed, and I had some money left over to pay bills.

The African Bedroom

I am definitely not a morning person. When I wake up, I'm really groggy. I place my alarm clock across the room so that I have to get out of bed to turn it off. I built my alarm clock from a kit sold by a company called Heathkit. They package the components and a printed circuit board, along with step-by-step instructions for assembling the gadget. I really enjoyed building these electronic items. I liked soldering all the components and wires into the correct spots on the printed circuit board—and then having something useful when it was done. I even built a color television and a microwave oven for my parents from Heathkits. The best thing about this alarm clock is that the alarm is not a continuous sound but an intermittent buzz. If an alarm makes a continuous tone, I just sleep through it. But the buzz-buzz-buzz cannot be ignored.

One morning I heard the annoying sound, climbed out of bed, and staggered across the room in the dark to turn off the offending alarm. As I reached for it, I knocked something off the dresser. I turned on the lights and looked at the floor. There I found a wooden statue of a giraffe nursing its baby. It had been carved from a single piece of wood. It was really beautiful. But I did not buy it and had no idea where it came from.

My bedroom has an African theme. The wallpaper is made up of leopards. On the walls are many things I brought back from Africa. I have masks, paintings, statues, and carved animals. So the giraffe statue fit my bedroom perfectly, even if I had never seen it before. By this time I was getting used to things magically appearing. At least, this was a big improvement over half a bag of chocolate chips! My list was growing: Khonsu, taxicab, chocolate chips, sushi, slot machine money, and a statue of a giraffe nursing its baby.

My first reaction was to invent a rational explanation for these mysterious appearances. I have a fertile imagination, but I could not think of any way to explain Khonsu and the taxicab. The sushi was real—I ate it! Sean's tooth got fixed by money from a slot machine in a place I didn't even want to visit. The statue of the giraffe that I never bought is still in my bedroom.

These odd events reminded me of the time I took a college course in physics because it was the only science course that fit my schedule. I had to study quantum mechanics in a class full of physics majors. If you've ever looked into this field, you'll find that it makes no rational sense. Particles disappear in one place and appear in another place without passing through the space between them. Maybe because I have a good imagination, I had no particular problem accepting a world that behaves in this way. I ended up with higher grades than many of the science majors who wanted the world to be more concrete, more rational. In the end, my overall reaction to these amazing experiences was one of great amusement and great curiosity. It was as though the quantum world was showing off in front of me.

The Message from Pat McKenna

I had gotten to know John Holland on the cruise with my mother; He gave me his email address, and I kept in touch. When I learned that John was appearing at a venue in New Hampshire featuring five mediums on May 18, 2002, I decided to go. This trip would be doubly important to me, both for what happened at the demonstration, and also because I met the person who would become the great love of my life. That part of the story will be told in another chapter.

The night before the demonstration, one of the featured mediums lost his wife in an auto accident. Obviously he was too upset to attend. Pat McKenna, a medium from Cape Cod, filled in at the last moment.

There were about 300 people in the audience. Pat McKenna opened the meeting with a prayer that drew upon her native American background, which I found very touching.

John Holland led off the first demonstration. He was brilliant as I expected. Now that I do public demonstrations myself, I realize how difficult it is to work with such a large crowd. The information has to be very specific in order to find the one person for whom the message from the spirit world is intended. John finished and then we had a short bathroom and coffee break.

Next another medium demonstrated "spirit art." In this process she drew sketches of the spirit while giving information about him or her. A camera was positioned over her shoulder so that we could see what she was drawing on a large screen. Between the drawing and the information coming verbally, audience members easily identified the person. It demonstrated another method by which our spirit friends and family can transmit information.

After another short break, it was Pat McKenna's turn. She picked out members of the audience and gave them short messages. When her time was up, she told the moderator that she needed to do one more. She walked down the aisle and stood directly in front of me. "I have never seen so many spirits around one person before, so I had to see this up close. Why aren't you on stage doing what I do? Your heart is so pure. Someday you will have the opportunity to hang out your own shingle, and you need to do that." I didn't know what to think or what to say. I could not see nor was I aware of all the spirits she saw, and doing what she had done was not even a remote fantasy with me. All the people seated around me were staring at me. I felt a little embarrassed by the attention.

At the break I talked to John Holland about this. He was as

surprised as I was by what had happened. I wanted to know more; I wanted a further explanation. Was this the mark of Khonsu at work again? I had no way of knowing.

I decided to track down Pat McKenna and arrange a private meeting with her. I was able to do so. On January 10, 2003, I drove to her home on Cape Cod. Her reading was not about linking me with my family and friends in the spirit world. Instead, it was about my life. She constructed a story that began before I was born and stepped through time. The session was recorded, so I can give you some of the things she told me—things that made sense to me and explained many of the experiences I had while growing up.

Pat is an engaging, very positive person who laughs a lot, especially when she sees something that she has never seen before. She sees what she calls "picture metaphors"—images and words forming in her mind. She began by tracing my life to see where I was at the present time. She said that the path I was on was splitting in two. At the junction she saw a sign that said, "intuitive skills, re-owned skills, past life skills." Beyond that, she saw a large billboard that read, "Welcome *finally* to your life, John." She said that this lifetime was a reclamation or a "re-do" of other lifetimes.

She went on to say that from the time I turned seven years old, I didn't understand myself, recognized that nobody else understood me, and realized how sad and uncontrollable my life was going to be. She commented that I had many abilities and high intelligence, and that I could mold myself to fit in with both paupers and kings, but that I was afraid to show my real self because I had been crushed so many times growing up. I had no trouble agreeing with what Pat was saying.

She had an interesting view of my mother. She told me that in a prior lifetime, Mom was high-born into a patrician family. My birth in that life had been prophesized by shamans, and Mom knew that she would only have me until I walked and talked, at which time I would join others in the study of arcane and occult matters. Early on, Mom felt that she lost me, because so many other people laid claim to me. So in this lifetime mom wanted to box me in. She felt that if she chased after me and yelled loud enough, she could control me. Pat said that she was sorry to have to say that, because it was very detrimental to my well-being. It explained a lot about my relationship with my mother in this lifetime, which I will discuss in a later chapter.

As for my father, Pat said that he wanted me to think like he did. He also thought that if he could control me, then everything would be okay. She said that he issued commands "when he was around long enough to give me those words." I found that comment interesting. For years Dad had been a traveling salesman. He'd leave home on Sunday evening and return Thursday afternoon. So he was not around a lot of the time. When Pat looked at my father through my eyes, all she saw was sadness. When she looked at my mother through my eyes, she said "run like hell!" and laughed. She commented that I had been emotionally blocked by both parents, and consequently learned to hide.

Pat said that the first twenty-one years of my life were really difficult, and those grim times had become my stumbling block. She told me that I knew that I would not fit in with my peers, that I didn't know where I belonged, but at the same time I had a sense that my life was being guided. I laughed when she commented that I had a tendency to overthink everything. How true! But at this stage of my life, she felt that I was finally following the guidance I was being given. Then Pat shared a great insight. When you think you don't fit in, she said, your tendency is to think that you're not as good as other people. The better approach is to admit that you don't fit in, you never will, and the hell with it! She drew the analogy of a pyramid. Most people are on the lower layers. As you go up higher on the pyramid, there are fewer and fewer people. I liked that image. She invited me to join the other crazies closer to the top of the pyramid. I had to laugh, but it was very reassuring.

During our tour of Egypt, Caroline Myss was working on a book called *Sacred Contracts*. Her concept is that we all come into this world with a mission, and also with the agreement to face serious obstacles that we have to overcome. Her idea stuck with me, and I asked Pat about my own "contract." She replied that I was a promoter of souls, explaining that I like to sponsor, promote, and befriend other people to make them go as far as they can go, that I have a far vision for others. I replied, "Yeah, that's me." Pat's final comment was that I needed to learn to express rage and anger. I'm really very easy going, and seldom get angry. Perhaps, she suggested, I hold it all in because I'm afraid to show my genuine feelings. The session gave me a lot to think about.

Pat invited me to return the next day for an informal workshop with six or seven ladies that she had invited to attend. I was more than happy to go. She gave me a chance to test my skill. She had the ladies stand up side by side. Then she asked me to try to get some information from each person, moving down the line from person to person. I had no idea how to do this. Pat suggested that I might try holding each woman's hands for a few seconds before saying whatever I was feeling.

I felt really silly doing this. I took the first lady's hands, and just started talking. "You work with papers in a place like a law office. You don't like your boss. You're looking for a new job. You will get an offer soon, and you'll be moving to another town. By the way, how's your left ankle?" It felt like somebody else was using my voice, because nothing that I said was premeditated. The words just came tumbling out.

While I'm saying all these things, Pat was standing behind me laughing and laughing. "So you're the person who can't do this!"

The lady was surprised at how accurate my information was. She told me that she did work for a law firm, but she was looking for a new job. Moreover, she had indeed broken her left ankle skiing. I moved down the line to the next lady and got similar results.

Pat was gloating that she had been right about me. I started to realize that I did have this strange ability. But what did it mean, and where would it lead?

A Workshop with John Holland

The next step in my adventure came in August 2003, seven months after my sessions with Pat McKenna. John Holland was offering a weekend workshop aimed at exploring and developing any psychic abilities the attendees might have. I decided to sign up because I had done so well at Pat McKenna's session, and I was curious to know what else I could do.

The meeting was held at a hotel in Andover, Massachusetts. There were about thirty people attending. John talked to us about how information comes to him and told us about his background. Then he had us try many different things. I did well on several of the experiments, but one made the biggest impression on me. John asked us to pair up with a stranger. My partner was seated in front of me while I stood behind her and rested my hands on her shoulders. The challenge was to "get" the happiest and saddest incidents in her life. I closed my eyes and began to get images in my imagination. Two particular incidents came to mind. I told her what I was experiencing. Both incidents were correct.

John then told us about his time in England, especially his experience at the Arthur Findlay College (AFC). Later, he suggested that I look into this. AFC is the foremost institution in the world for the study of psychic science. I wrote down the name, but I did not follow up on his suggestion for some time. Still, I left the weekend knowing that I could do things that I could never have imagined doing a few months earlier.

Glenn Klausner and the Mysterious 14th

Pat McKenna had told me that the changes in my life would come rapidly. She was right. A month later I went with my mother on our annual cruise. When we returned to her home in Lehigh Acres, Florida, I recalled that a medium I had heard about was living in Fort Myers. I decided to look him up. I called his office and was told that he was booked solid—except there just happened to be a cancellation for the next day. I booked an appointment. By this time I expected the Universe to pull strings for me, so the convenient cancellation was not that surprising.

On September 19, Mom and I drove to Fort Myers for a private sitting with Glenn Klausner, who was located in a regular office building. He was a handsome man, much younger than I expected. He met us and had us sit down in his office. Glenn sat behind his desk, while Mom and I sat in chairs opposite him.

After learning our names, he started immediately. I recently transcribed the recording of this session and can quote Glenn exactly. "There's another John apparently in this room, as a spirit, that's coming off more a father, husband figure to you." Of course, he was talking about my father.

Glenn described how Dad passed and then continued. "Your dad wanted me to tell you he wants you to know how very proud of you he is. He has come to a much higher spiritual realization of things that he couldn't understand when he was physically alive and in relationship with you. ... But he makes me feel like he kind of doesn't understand, like I don't know if you butted heads sometimes with him—like if you said something to your dad, your dad is going forty miles in a different direction than you. He says he understands that now. The reason that he butted heads with you was part of a soul challenge not only to him but to you as well. ... He said the one thing he regrets in your relationship with him is that he didn't tell you how much he was proud of you, even of your smallest accomplishments or biggest ones—to recognize you as a soul more often."

I felt good about what Glenn had just said. My relationship with Dad was so dramatic that it had to be some kind of soul challenge. I'm just happy that we worked it out in this lifetime. God forbid I should have to come back and do that all over again; once was enough! Yet the biggest surprise was yet to come.

Glenn asked us if we had any questions. I asked about my career. Things had been very slow in the engineering world. Glenn replied, "He (Dad) said you have two different things going on. One, like he keeps showing me the word Microsoft for some reason." I told Glenn that I was involved with a software company. "And he said another thing. Your experience with John Holland or knowing John Holland has either opened or is going to continue to open another door within you spiritually. He says that—I don't know if John (Holland) told you this, that you have mediumistic ability yourself. Then he says—he keeps saying mediumistic … opening to channel." That was a shocker. Dad had always ridiculed Mom's interest in psychics.

Glenn continued. "He says you're kind of in a flux, not sure where to fit. 14. All I know is he keeps saying the number 14. He says 14th. He put 'th' after it. So maybe like the 14th of a month."

Neither Glenn nor I had any idea what this meant, and Dad would not explain it. I asked Glenn to ask Dad about my aeronautical engineering work. Glenn replied, "He says that the Universe has other plans for you. … And he says that the ones you've already come into contact with have given you sort of little pieces of it here and there, like John Holland, even what he apparently conveyed to me about mediumistic ability. He says that all these experiences of yours are being cultivated."

I asked again about the role that engineering would have in my future. Dad said it was okay but only as a kind of "hobby." I have to say that Dad is the last person I would ever expect to be talking about spirituality or mediumship. He was an earthy jock who was not particularly intellectual, though he was certainly intelligent.

The reading with Glenn confirmed what Pat McKenna had said in both the New Hampshire auditorium and in her home.

I was beginning to believe in my mission, but even if I accepted what others were saying about me, I had absolutely no idea where to go or what to do about it. One thing that was a total mystery to me was the number 14. What on earth could that mean? Dad had repeated it several times. It had to mean something.

The answer came two months later, in November. I got a phone call from Sheree, a lady in New England who ran a meditation group to which my new acquaintance belonged. She asked me if I was going to New York for a weekend workshop with John Edward. For months I had been watching the television program, *Crossing Over.* John was a medium, and the show documented his work with a studio audience consisting of around sixty people. The way he got such specific information impressed me. Sheree suggested that we could meet for lunch or dinner there.

Until her phone call, I had no idea that John Edward was giving a workshop on mediumship. It sounded really interesting so I checked his website and called the reservation number, only to learn that the workshop had been sold out for months. Still, something seemed rather strange about this phone call from Sheree.

It was out of the blue. I didn't even know her.

Sure enough, a week before the workshop, Sheree called me again. She had a friend who had planned to go with her, but at the last minute her friend couldn't go. Would I like to buy her ticket? Yes! So on November 14th I flew to Providence, and Sheree drove us to New York City. The 14th! What more proof could I ask for! I couldn't help remembering my father's words that all these experiences were being cultivated. The way this trip had unfolded was a perfect illustration of that.

The workshop with John Edward was impressive, but I was bothered by the fact that he had two bodyguards with him. One stood near him in the front of the room. The other one stood behind us. John's life had been threatened by people who, for some reason, believed that his work was some kind of evil black magic. How sad.

John was very funny. He asked us, "How many people here think they're as psychic as a rock?" A lot of hands went up. John said that most people are capable of picking up information psychically, but they never learned to do it.

John had us doing exercises as well as listening to him. He made us pair up with the person seated behind us. The goal was to tell that person as much as we could about them. By this time, I had no problem at all doing this. I told this lady where she lived, how many kids she had, about her love of the ocean, and where she worked. I found that I could do all the exercises he asked us to do.

After the workshop ended, John had some gifts for us, and patiently signed books. He impressed me as a very down-to-earth person, humble and funny, a man who wanted everyone to recognize his or her own capabilities. He was definitely not a stuck-up television star.

Sheree drove us back to Providence. I had a plane to catch. However, the plane was delayed. We finally landed in Detroit, where I had to change to a flight to South Bend. Because of the delay, the last flight to South Bend had already departed. The airline offered me a coupon for a free hotel and a meal voucher, which I was grateful for.

I went outside to catch the courtesy van to the hotel. It was raining. I climbed into the van and sat next to a young lady on the wide bench seat behind the driver. I made the comment that I hoped she was having a better day than I was, having missed my flight home. She countered that she had flown in from Texas, and the airline had lost her bag. She was a flight attendant who had to go to work the next morning, and her uniform was in the lost bag.

Instantly, I had an image pop into my head, and I couldn't help explore it a bit. "Is it a green plaid bag with a black handle?" I asked.

She looked at me quizzically, and replied, "No, I have that one. It's in the back."

She slid a bit further from me.

"Oh", I said, "then it must be the black bag."

"Black and what other color?" she asked, while sliding further away.

"Black and red," I replied without hesitation.

By now she had slid as far away from me as possible — and was pinned against the side of the van. "Okay, smarty, when will I get the bag?"

Without thinking, I said "11:19." She told me that the next flight from Texas was due in at 10:50. I thought to myself, well, by the time they get the bags off the plane and over to the hotel, it sounded about right. I have no idea whether that prediction turned out to be true, but I would not be surprised at all to learn that it was exactly correct.

However, I had not been able to reclaim my bag either. I checked in, went to my room, and sprawled out on the bed staring at the ceiling. I started reviewing all the things that had happened to me. I accepted the conclusion that all these experiences seemed planned up to this point. The whole thing about the 14th was proof of that. Even this unexpected night in Detroit might have been planned. Had I gotten home on time, I'd be busy looking at my mail and email and listening to any voicemails. Being stuck here for the night gave me time to think. I decided that it was time to embrace these new skills and see where it would lead.

So on a rainy night in Detroit, I decided to take John Holland's suggestion, and apply to the Arthur Findlay College in Stansted, England. The day after I arrived home, I found their website and put down deposits on two courses.

BOOK TWO
Educating Myself

Chapter 3

Training at the Real Hogwarts

I ARRIVED IN LONDON on February 28, 2004. I was not a stranger to London; I had been there several times. In November, 1999, I was honored by the Guild of Air Pilots and Air Navigators at a gala banquet at Guildhall in the old city of London. This impressive building had been built more than fifty years before Columbus came to the Americas. No one does pomp and pageantry better than the British, and the many courses, toasts, and ceremonies at the dinner were truly memorable. I was awarded a medal from His Royal Highness Prince Philip, who serves as the Grand Master of the Guild, due to his long involvement in aviation. The medal was given to honor the design of an airplane called the Eagle X-TS, which had started an aviation industry in Western Australia. Australia is a member of the Commonwealth Realm, with Queen Elizabeth II as its monarch.

I had brought my niece Allyson with me to celebrate her seventeenth birthday. She loves the theater, and so we saw *Les Miserables, Phantom of the Opera,* and *The Lion King* while we were there. We also went out to see Stonehenge and the Roman city of Bath. It was her first time out of the country. Children grow up so quickly, and this was my one chance to spend a lot of time with her and really get to know her.

This time I was alone. I planned to study at what I'm calling the "Real Hogwarts," and I was wondering what sorts of challenges awaited me. I had decided to come a day early and spend a night in London first, because flights from Chicago leave late at night and arrive very early in the morning due to the time change involved, and I didn't want to show up at the school half asleep. I took the tube (subway) from Heathrow to the Tower of London exit. My hotel was right across from the Tower Bridge, near many historic sites. My course would begin the next day, February 29. I thought it was an interesting coincidence that the start of this new adventure would begin on a rare date that only comes around once every four years. The next morning I took a train to the Stansted airport and then a taxi to the college. The driver called it "Spook's Hall." I wasn't sure what to make of that.

The Arthur Findlay College (AFC) is a large, beautiful mansion set in the English countryside. It looks like something you might see in a movie. Next door there is a horse ranch. Cows often come up to the fence marking the limits of the grounds. The mansion was constructed between 1871 and 1876 by Mr. William Fuller-Maitland, who unfortunately passed away before it was completed. His son resided in the mansion until 1921, when it was sold to Sir Albert Ball. Two years later J. Arthur Findlay and his wife Gertrude visited the estate and decided to buy it. They moved into the mansion in 1926.

During the Second World War, the Findlays loaned the estate to the Ministry of Defence for use as a hospital. More than 5,000 soldiers passed through the facility. After the war the family moved back into the mansion. Arthur Findlay wanted to establish an institution for the pursuit of knowledge about the psychic world and mediumship, so in 1964 he conveyed the estate to the Spiritualist National Union (SNU). In England there are many Spiritualist churches, and the denomination has equal standing with other religious denominations, such as Presbyterian or Lutheran. The Deed of Gift gave the SNU 15,750 acres of land along with the main mansion and all its outlying buildings.

The SNU had to remodel the upper floors, installing electricity and heat—and constructing bedrooms and bathrooms for the students. When you walk inside you are greeted by the grandeur of a place that obviously had housed very wealthy people. In 1999 an addition called the Sanctuary was completed. Spiritualist services are held there twice a week, and it is also used for classes. This can't be England without a pub, so in 2006 the small pub area was enlarged and can now hold about sixty people. The bar opens at 9:00 P.M. after the last class ends.

I called this the Real Hogwarts for a reason. In the fabulous Harry Potter books by J. K. Rowling the magic is imaginary. In Stansted Hall, however, what goes on is real magic. One of the characteristics of the fictional Hogwarts is that there are many confusing staircases. This fits Stansted Hall too. Finding your way around is a challenge at first. Open a door and you'll find yet another corridor and staircase leading who knows where. I thought I had them all figured out after five or six courses, but then I was assigned a room in a wing that I didn't even know existed! Up a back staircase, through two doors, down a staircase, turn, up another staircase, turn, through another door, turn and there was my room. I drew a map so that I could find my way back. On check-in days, I tried to help new arrivals find their rooms. Bathrooms are shared, so I usually showered in the middle of the day when I didn't have to wait in line (or queue up, as the British say).

The Adventure Begins

When I checked in, I had to use a small printed map to find my room, where I met my roommate Phil, who was from Toronto. At 4:30 P.M. we went to the Sanctuary for our first session. The course I was attending was called "Mediumship Development and Training" and led by a well-known British medium, Glyn Edwards. Glyn was in a good mood and displayed his great sense of humor in spite of the partial paralysis on one side of his face. He talked about how we need to understand our own power, and that spirits want to communicate with us and want us to hear them.

Later I asked Phil what he thought was the most important thing Glyn had said. Phil thought that the joy and enthusiasm of being able to connect to Spirit was the most important thing. Glyn had also pointed out that we need to notice what is happening inside us — how we're getting the information — because understanding this gives us some control over it.

In all the courses at the college, the students are divided into groups based on their experience and interests. Being new, I was placed in the beginner's group of ten people under the tutelage of Sue Taylor. The different groups met in various parts of the mansion: the library, the large lounge, the lecture room, the blue room, the Sanctuary, the conference room, the attic, or the Pioneer Centre. Our group met in the Pioneer Centre, where energy healing takes place on certain days of the week.

The schedule each day was to meet with our groups from 9:00 to 10:30 each morning, followed by a tea break (this is England, after all), then again from 11:00 to 1:00, at which time we ate lunch in the dining room. Actually the food was pretty good. Back to our groups at 2:30 until 4:00, another tea break, then again from 4:30 to 6:00 when we had our dinner. The final session was often held with all the groups joining together, and that session ran from 7:30 until 9:00. It was a long day, the work was intense, and after a lemonade in the pub I was ready for bed.

Glyn was a proponent of a type of meditation called "sitting in the power." All the groups began each day with this practice: thirty minutes sitting still and not moving a muscle. The first day my mind ran wild. I thought about how my house was doing, whether my car was safe in the parking lot, whether I had turned off the coffee pot, and every other distraction my mind could invent. Thirty minutes seemed like an eternity. Back at home I have a very spiritual friend, Lem Joyner, who had taught me the trick of putting each distracting thought into a helium balloon and then releasing it. I used a lot of balloons on that first day! By the end of the week, though, my monkey mind finally surrendered, and I actually craved the stillness.

One of the phrases I heard a lot at AFC was "stepping into the power." I never understood what this meant until I asked Simon James, another course organizer. He said it's like a fish becoming aware of the water. Somehow that made sense to me. We are usually aware of our own bodies and minds, but we are less aware of the air and the environment around us. So sitting in the power means that we expand our awareness to everything around us while sitting motionless in a chair.

After the meditation period, Sue paired us up and we tried to "read" our partners for the first time. My notes say that I "got" the great-grandmother of the lady I was paired with, along with the first letter of her name, her age, house, garden, and the fact that her husband met her when she crossed over. I was very pleased with that

The next challenge was to get three facts about a deceased person for someone in our group: sex, father or mother's side, and age at death. I reported a man—from someone's mother's side—who died at seventy-two from lung cancer. I said that he worked underground and hated that. An Irish lady said it was all true, except that it was her husband's father. The details were correct, but I got the relationship wrong.

Our group spent the week experimenting with various ways of getting information. We drew pictures, and our partner would tell us about our lives by interpreting the energy in the pictures. Another time, we picked an object from a huge pile Sue had placed in the middle of the room, then tried to say something about each person based on the object he or she had chosen.

We also tried a light trance state. This is a deeper meditation, in which you lose awareness of your body, empty your mind and listen. Our task was to hear some kind of philosophical statement that we could then share with the group. After a while, I found myself kind of floating in an empty dark place and heard these words: "God does not need to be worshipped. God does not need validation." That surprised me. From the time I was in first grade we started our day in church with the Catholic mass. Isn't the whole point to worship God? But finally I realized that any intelligence that could have imagined, designed, and created this universe could not possibly have any self-esteem problems and need constant reassurance. It did make sense. Then I got the phrase, "The journey is the destination." That idea was less foreign. Our lives are journeys whose destinations may never be known. I've met hundreds of other students like me at the college who as children had never said, "I'm going to be a medium when I grow up and talk to dead people." So I embrace this journey with all the joy and grief I've experienced along the way.

On Wednesday we joined Glyn's group of advanced students for the sitting-in-the power meditation. After that, Glyn asked us to do healing. He asked me to work with Nicola, who had undergone a heart-lung transplant. The process of healing involves letting energy flow through you to the recipient. I could feel that energy, and Nicola said she felt it too.

On Thursday I was paired with a lady named Justine. I got her cousin, who died from leukemia. I felt her physical pain. Then I got her emotional pain. She had a two-year-old-son, and her husband had been cheating on her. Now she knew she was dying and would have to leave her little boy with this man whom she no longer loved or trusted. The emotions overwhelmed me completely, and I collapsed. I felt trapped in all this pain and sadness. Sue came over and placed her hand on my back to break the link. Afterwards we had a long talk. While it is good and even necessary to feel the spirit, we cannot become trapped in those feelings. Sue gave me a lot of suggestions on how to prevent this kind of thing, which I have found very helpful.

In another session, we paired up again with the goal of telling our partner something about the past, present, and future. Edward, my partner for this task, told me that I was spot on. After a tea break, it was Edward's turn. He told me that he felt all the pain I've undergone in my life, and it almost made him cry. Afterwards, each of us tried to get a link to a spirit for someone in our group. I got a man who died in an auto accident. He had been boating on a river earlier and was on his way home. I described his injuries and said that he had died before he could be pulled from the wreckage. It was our tutor Sue's husband. It must have been hard for her to hear this while having to control her true emotions. I felt sorry for her.

The next day we tried another experiment. Half of the group sat facing the wall, and then someone sat behind each of us. We were to say who was behind us and then give them a message. I thought I had Bernie behind me, and I got a lot of information about the battle in the Falkland Islands. I was wrong; Karl-Heinz was behind me. Later I asked Bernie about what I had said, and he knew exactly what I was talking about. Oh well.

The closing session was held with Glyn in the Sanctuary. He told us how magnificent we all were—and to never let anyone tell us otherwise. He reminded us that the spirit world needs us in order to communicate with their loved ones and that the spirits are very grateful for our hard work. I had never thought of it in that way, but it made sense. I've often thought that the college is surrounded by spirits who are there to work with us to perfect our skills.

As I was walking past the grand staircase, Glyn was coming down the stairs. He stopped me and told me that he was going to be in Boston in the spring. He gave me a phone number and said he'd like me to meet him there. Glyn is kind of a minor god in the college, so I was surprised and flattered by the invitation.

My journal entry for that evening says "I am incredibly tired and I'm glad that tomorrow is the last day, although I will miss Glyn."

The next morning most of the students left. I went into the small town of Mountfitchet to an internet site where I could check my email and let everyone know that I was really excited by my first week at the college. My next course didn't start until the next day, so several of us who were staying over went out to dinner at a local inn. I found out that restaurants in England are very expensive!

The Second Week

"Celebrate the Magic" began with private meetings with Simon James, the course organizer. We had filled out questionnaires ahead of time, and this information along with some small talk enabled him to assign us to the various groups. There were 108 students from fourteen countries attending the course. They ranged in age from twenty to ninety-plus. This is one of the most popular courses offered at the college.

At the opening session, the Sanctuary was dark. Then each of the four tutors came in, lit a candle, and spoke to us. Mavis Pittila, a living legend, touched me deeply. She said that sometimes we are not loved and are lonely and sad. We need to know that the spirit world loves us, and our goal is to feel the energy of their love for us. Simon told us that we need to find the joy in our lives. Being a medium isn't worth doing unless it makes us feel joyful in our lives.

Simon made several profound points. "Sensitivity is the price of sensitivity," he said. Like many other mediums, I am bothered by loud noises and the chatter in crowded rooms. It can be overwhelming. It takes great sensitivity to do the work we do, and the price we pay for that is being very sensitive to our environments.

Another time he said, "Here we all are, spending time with

people we don't know while talking to people who aren't even here!"

And another: "Why do we demonstrate in front of 500 people, but put us in a room with six people and we stare at the floor?" Simon had me pegged. I've traveled around the country as a Distinguished Lecturer for the American Institute of Aeronautics and Astronautics, speaking to hundreds of people. But put me in a room with a few strangers, and I hide in the corner.

Finally, this one: "We best serve the spirit world by being a light to the people around us."

The next morning the group assignments were posted on the bulletin board. I was pleased to be assigned to Mavis. Our group assembled in the Sanctuary. We introduced ourselves and talked about our experience in this field. I began to get nervous. All of the other people in our group had at least three years of experience. When it was my turn, I introduced myself then confessed that I had been doing this work for one week. The group just stared at me. She asked each of us why we wanted to be a medium. My reply was that the path chooses us and not the other way around. She liked that answer.

Mavis' group was all about platform demonstrations. Mediumship is a big part of a Spiritualist service, and the college is the training ground for these mediums. For the main part of the service, one or more mediums stand up front and bring messages for people in the congregation from their family and friends in the spirit world. We were going to be practicing this. I was already terrified, but then Mavis told me that I'd be first. I suspected that she wanted to kick me out of her group as quickly as possible. I walked up to the front and stood facing the congregation. Fortunately, I got a link with a man named Richard, which turned out to be a good reading for a lady in the group. However, Mavis complained that I would get a piece of information, then stop and analyze it, then get another piece, and so on. She told me to stop thinking and analyzing and just go with the flow. You have no idea how hard it is for an engineer to stop thinking and analyzing things! Those are the very skills that made me a successful engineer. Now they were preventing me from being a successful medium. Nonetheless I remained in the group, so I must have passed her test.

After that session, I made a note in my journal: "If I have any hope of doing this work, this week is going to be vital in my development. I'm really glad that I'm here.☺" After lunch a lady from Florida stopped me to say that I did a good job that morning. It made me feel wonderful.

We did quite a few exercises during the week. Mavis had a lady sit in a chair in the front of the room, and we tried to answer a list of questions about her. During the evening lecture, she had a few props for us. The first was a small tray filled with sand. She asked Lana, a lady from another group, to press her handprints into the sand. I thought to myself, what's that all about? Then Mavis said "Now John will come up and tell you the story of your life up to the age of twenty by looking at the sand." Whoa! I thought this was ridiculous. Surely I'll be humiliated in front of the whole school. Why is Mavis out to get me?

I went up front and looked at the handprints in the sand, took a deep breath and started talking. She had an older sister who picked on her. The family moved to another house when she was five. I talked about her friends, her school, her first boyfriend, and so on. Lana confirmed the things I had said. Mavis said simply, "Well done, John." I felt like I had just been knighted!

Another person came up front and swished her hands in a bowl of water, and the next student faced the same challenge that I had, this time by staring at the water. Several other methods were demonstrated. I learned that evening that information can come in many ways.

On Wednesday night, I woke up suddenly and jerked bolt upright as though I had been struck by lightning. The reality of what

I had been doing had hit me for the first time. I was talking to dead people. These people are dead! It may seem silly that it took a week-and-a-half to sink in. But until that moment all I was trying to do was to complete the exercises my tutors gave us without falling flat on my face. From that moment I would never be the same.

The Acid Test

Thursday morning Mavis gave us another test. We were to stand on the platform with our backs to the group while everyone moved to a different chair. We were to get a spirit and specific information. If someone recognized the person, they would raise their hand so that Mavis could see it. For each piece of information the recipient would shake their head yes or no. Mavis would then relay the response by whispering "yes" or yelling "NO!" When we finished, we were to say where the recipient was seated.

The terror of the first day returned. How am I supposed to know where someone was seated, when I couldn't see them and they couldn't speak? Fortunately, I wasn't the first person called up, so I could watch how my classmates handled the challenge. Finally, it was my turn. I said that this was a man who had been a high school sweetheart, and it went back many years. The man used to bring flowers, but he was laughing about it, so there had to be something funny about the flowers. Mavis whispered, "yes." It turned out to be a great reading, even though I didn't know who I was talking to. When it came time to pick out a chair, I realized that I didn't need to know because the spirit of this man certainly knew and would guide me. First, I asked in my mind whether the person was seated on the left or right of the center aisle. Then I pictured the first row, then the second, and so on until I felt a confirmation from the spirit. Then I started counting chairs from the aisle until I felt a confirmation. The correct classmate was seated on the right side of the Sanctuary in the first seat on the aisle in the third row. Yes! I felt like setting off fireworks and opening a bottle of champagne. Later, a lady came up to me and thanked me for bringing her old friend through. She told me that she had been hoping to hear from him all week and said that she would know it was truly him if he talked about the flowers. He used to steal them from neighbor's yards. He had died from a disease, which I also mentioned.

My journal from this session contains several memorable quotes. "The next time you feel you have to defend something about yourself, ask yourself 'why am I feeling I must defend this?'"

Another good quote: "Another person can only trigger pain when there is already pain within. ... If there's no pain within, another cannot bring it out. You would only feel compassionate and sorry for him, not angry and threatened."

At the end of the course, my head was overflowing with information. The closing ceremony had the students walking one by one into the dark Sanctuary. Each of the tutors put their hands on us as we walked by. Then we lit a candle and sat down. A lady from Vancouver sang a song for us. The lyrics began "The work we do is holy. Holy are we." It was very moving, and there were lots of hugs and tears when it ended. The tutors are extraordinary teachers, and I had learned a lot, done a lot, and gained a lot of confidence.

My last experience was very funny. The college has a tiny elevator (the British call it a lift) and Saturday morning four of us crammed ourselves and our luggage into this tiny space. The lady closest to the buttons seemed frozen on what to do. One of the other ladies called out, "Just step into the power, Dear, and push the first button that comes to mind."

Two Years Later

My next trip to the college was in March 2006, two years after my first courses there. I was at a place in my life where I really needed to be in a house full of mediums. I'm going to leave that part of the story for another chapter.

My tutor was Simone Key, whom I quickly learned to love. She has a beautiful face, framed by thick, black hair. To me, she has a regal air about her, even though she's one of the most down-to-earth people I know. She had an amazing story to tell. She had been raised as an atheist and had no beliefs or interest in any kind of spiritual world. Then in a very short time mediumistic and psychic abilities just appeared. Eventually, she decided to seek out a Spiritualist church to try and sort out what she was experiencing.

In England most mediums are trained in small groups that meet in circles every week at the same time. The members try to link with a spirit, receive a message and convey the information to the other group members. There are certain rituals involved that vary from group to group, like lighting a candle or having flowers in the room. These things were thought to be necessary for the process to occur.

So here comes Simone, who had all these abilities without any training. She was kicked out of the first circle she joined because she said you don't need any special rituals to link with spirit. Simone found another circle and continued her work with the Spiritualist National Union. She is now a minister.

Simone tells it like it is. She cuts away all the b.s. about the work we do. One of my favorite stories about her is that people kept telling her that she needed to learn her spirit guide's name. For a while, she would meditate and keep asking for a name. One day she finally got her answer. She heard a loud voice say, "Chop Suey Louie." It was the spirit world's way of telling her that the whole issue was silly. I have to say that while I am aware of a group of spirits working with me, I have never learned any names. Maybe they never had names. I just call them "my team." So Simone's story was a relief.

Simone taught us that we can trust the spirit world completely and that we can put the burden of getting information on them, instead of feeling like we are pulling teeth. For example, you could say, "He's telling me that he died from ..." without having any idea of how the man died. What happens is that when you reach the end of the sentence, the spirit will fill in the blank. This takes a tremendous amount of trust. Nobody wants to look stupid, and it is really hard to say something like that without knowing the answer in advance. I keep working on it, and it has always worked for me. I can truly say that the spirit world has never let me down.

Simone is also an expert in trance, so we did exercises to explore this. In a trance state we stop feeling our bodies, lose awareness of everything around us, and become more attuned to our minds. I enjoy that feeling. Simone observed the energy fields around us while we were doing this and then commented on what she observed. She told me that I had the spirit world pushing me forward and that it was time to come forward and be recognized. She also said that I could become a trance speaker. This is a process of turning your body over to a spirit master who can then speak through you.

Simone told us that we are the modern alchemists. Instead of turning base metals into gold, we are transforming ourselves. However, developing our power also makes us a kind of alien. She believes that this power comes from our own souls and that we're not learning to do it but just remembering it.

Paul Jacobs gave us a lecture about colors. I was interested in this because at the time I already sensed a cocoon of energy around living things. I especially enjoy watching the auras around the trees in my back yard. Usually they are a light gray color, but it is also possible to feel colors. At first I doubted this. We did an exercise where a man sat in a chair in front of us, and we had to write down a list of colors starting at the skin and going outwards. I didn't see any colors, so I tried to feel them. Once again it felt like I was making the whole thing up. Then we compared notes. Both the student to my left and the one to my right had written down the same colors in the same order! Hmmm. Maybe it wasn't make-believe after all.

Thelma, another tutor, had a special camera that can record the colors around a person. She took a picture of me and interpreted the colors. She also showed the effect on the colors if you hold a quartz crystal. It's amazing how they change. I'm only recently learning about crystals, but based on the evidence I've seen, I do think they can alter the energy fields around us and, in that way, affect our health and our attitudes.

Simon set up an interesting experiment involving energy. Two people sat opposite each other and tried to build up their energy. Then a third person would walk between us. When it was my turn to try this, I definitely felt the energy field between my classmates. Simon also wanted us to realize that we are serving not only the individual spirits but also the Creator. "When we reach out to a spirit, a hand reaches back to us ... the hand of the Creator. When we prove existence beyond death, we are proving the existence of a divine being. We work for God." We needed to hear that. We are so caught up in the techniques and demands of this work that we lose sight of the big picture.

Most of the time during those two weeks, we were doing readings, either for a single person or for our group. Practice, practice, practice. One morning we went out to the long gallery and picked out a chair to sit in, and a new person would come every half hour for a reading. At the end of the morning session, all the people I had read for came back to give a critique. It is very helpful to get this kind of feedback. The afternoon session was all about platform demonstrations. Our tutors and classmates all wanted each of us to be the best we could be. So we were pushed beyond our comfort levels. If you got a first name, what was their last name? Where did they live? What was their house number? If we don't look for these things, we will never get them. The college provided the environment where we could try and fail. As they say, if you fall, you fall gently. But if you keep trying, eventually you can get these kinds of facts. Mavis Pittila even gets phone numbers!

I had one session with Jan Marshall. She is an artist, and she had us draw pictures of a spirit, then stand in front of our group with the picture and give information about the person we had drawn. I enjoyed doing that and was quite good at it.

Working from 8 A.M. to 9 P.M. every day takes its toll. My roommate was Dutch but was living in France. It gave me a chance to dust off my rusty French, and we became good friends. One morning Michel woke up and starting singing, "It's a hard day's night and I've been working like a dog." Then he muttered to himself, "spiritual concentration camp." I had to laugh.

Friday night Michel and I skipped dinner at the college and went to a local inn instead. We got back after all the doors had been locked. Since neither of us remembered to bring the codes for the locks, we had to search the grounds for an unlocked window. Michel squeezed inside and unlocked the door for me.

A Secret Meeting

Mary, a classmate from Scotland, asked to meet me privately in the large lounge one evening. We weren't supposed to give readings outside of class, but she felt she needed to do this. She said she had a link with someone named Jack. She said that he had an airplane with two wings, and I used to fly in it. She saw us flying over a lake. She even knew the registration number of the airplane! Mary said that Jack had died instantly while flying an airplane just before the airplane crashed. She also gave me the names of Jack's two sons who had preceded him in death.

I was really surprised and pleased to hear from Jack. He was a recovered alcoholic and heir to a fortune, who had been a pilot in World War II. His desire to return to flying was his primary motive to stop drinking. To have something to do, he opened a small independent gas station. His customers never suspected that the guy filling their tanks and washing their windshields was a multi-millionaire.

Jack had three airplanes: two antique Fleet biplanes and a Piper Comanche. He offered to take me flying on a regular basis one summer while I still lived with my parents. The one advantage to my odd sleeping arrangement was that I could leave without anyone hearing. He'd come to our house early in the morning, and we'd drive over to the Mishawaka Pilot's Club and get his 1924 Fleet biplane out of the hangar and fuel it up. The plane had two open cockpits. The roar of the radial engine and the smell of the oil were intoxicating for me.

Flying over newly plowed fields filled the air with the smell of earth. We'd fly at low altitudes over a few small lakes, waving at the fishermen. For breakfast, we'd land at a small airport with a coffee shop. Jack became a close confidant and a role model for me. Being with him canceled out a lot of the negativity in my life—and increased my love of airplanes.

A few years later Jack found a Ryan PT-A, which was the model he had learned to fly in, and bought it in order to restore it. He went to Florida to pick up the plane and fly it home. I will never forget the day my mother came to tell me that Jack had been found dead sitting in the airplane in a farmer's field in Georgia. I collapsed in tears and disbelief; I was inconsolable.

The autopsy showed that Jack had suffered a major heart attack. His face had been severely cut up by the windshield, and there was blood in the cabin. There was no detectable fuel in the tanks, and there was no damage to the plane.

Jack's friend Harry had a large Cessna 421 twin engine airplane and offered to fly to Georgia and pick up the body. He called my mother and asked if "John" would like to go with him. I took it to mean me, because Jack and I were so close. When I got to the airport and saw the surprise on Harry's face, I realized that he actually had wanted my father. We are both called John.

He agreed to take me anyway. We flew to a small airport in Georgia. Harry went inside to file a flight plan for the return trip. A hearse pulled up alongside the plane. The funeral home had hoped to sell the most expensive coffin in their inventory, figuring that anyone who owned an airplane must be rich. But we could not fit a coffin into the airplane and arranged to do without, so they didn't care what he looked like. They wheeled the gurney over to the steps of the plane and removed the sheet. Jack was almost naked, with thick black stitches sewn on his face and chest. I was horrified. I put my arms under his armpits and pulled him onto the airplane, then found a blanket to cover him up. Harry came back and we flew in silence back to Indiana. I had nightmares for months afterwards.

Mary told me that Jack was very proud of me—that I was "soaring" now. He was such an important person in my life that hearing from him made a huge impact on me. I was grateful not only to Mary, but for the whole process that makes this kind of communication possible.

Learning to Trust the Spirit World

For the next course, my tutor was Brenda Lawrence. Our homework was to get a link the night before our session, then decide who it was for and give them the message. This worked out well. We also tried a similar experiment. We drew a number and were asked to get a link for whoever the person was who had previously been assigned that number. That also worked out very well for me.

I used that same technique for a public demonstration at Sacred Waters, a venue for all kinds of spiritual activities located near my home. The night before the demonstration I wrote down the number one on a blank sheet of paper. Then I asked the spirit world to please talk to me if there was someone who wanted to give a message to the person who would draw number one. I wrote down all the information I received. I did the same thing for numbers two and three. The next night all the people who came drew slips of paper from a hat. Only three of them were marked with numbers; the rest were blank. I told the audience that if they drew a number, they shouldn't say anything to anyone. I read all the information I had for the first person. Then I asked who had drawn the number one. It was a man. It was his brother who had linked with me. I read every item on the list I had written, to make sure each detail was accurate. It was. I did the same thing for the lady who drew number two. I had her mother by name—and some details about her personality and family. Then I read the information for spirit number three. The lady who drew that number had no idea what I was talking about. However, the lady sitting next to her understood everything. She had been disowned by her mother, and while driving to Sacred Waters she kept saying, "I don't want a reading. I don't want a reading." But the spirit world had other ideas. That reading turned out to be the most important of the evening, because it reunited mother and daughter.

What I proved that evening was that the spirit world knew ahead of time who was going to come to the public demonstration and who would draw each number. This seems impossible until you realize that in the spirit world there is no time. From that perspective they see things that are in the future in our physical world.

I also used another technique that Brenda taught me. I sat down and was blindfolded, and the hat was passed around again. This time only one slip of paper was marked with a star. The person who drew the star came and sat opposite me but was not allowed to speak. They could shake their heads "yes" or "no", and the rest of the audience would relay that to me. This also works well. I don't need to know who is sitting there, because the spirit who links with me definitely knows the person. I got this lady's mother, her devotion to St. Teresa, and other specific information.

I wanted to prove that the work I do is not based on body language or by using a bunch of guesses and hoping for a hit.

The Trance Course

When my nephew Ian turned seventeen, I decided to bring him with me to the college. I had watched him grow up and sensed that he had a lot of psychic ability. I wanted him to know what he was capable of doing, because that would change the way he thought about himself and affect his future. I found a week that had one course for beginners and another course that focused on trance. It was Ian's first trip outside the country. Mike Mangold, an American Airlines captain, gave us tickets to London. I had designed some modifications to Mike's airplane, with which he won the World Championship in the Red Bull Air Races. We ended up in Business Class on the way to London and First Class on the way back to Chicago. I told Ian he was spoiled for life.

The trance course was organized by Simone Key. Of all the tutors I've been with, she has been the most influential in my development. One day she was lecturing, and I saw her transform into an Egyptian queen, like the ones whose statues I had seen in the Cairo Museum. I was so struck by this that I told her afterwards what I had seen. I was surprised when she told me that her mother was Egyptian.

One morning we had an interesting assignment. We were to ask a question about something that disturbed us, then go into a trance state looking for an answer. I had been concerned about the trend that was pulling people apart. The gap between the rich and the rest of us had been growing wider. American culture was dividing into small groups who attacked each other. Sunnis and Shias were killing each other. The human race seemed consumed with amplifying differences rather than finding common ground. Political and religious differences were creating pockets of true hatred. I wanted to know why this was happening.

After a while I dropped into a state that feels like pure awareness floating in empty space. I've always enjoyed this feeling. Then
I saw the symbol for Pisces, which shows two fish swimming in
opposite directions. I understood that we are moving out of the
age of Pisces into the age of Aquarius. These ages are long spans
of time that have different focuses. Prior to the age of Pisces, we
passed through the age of Aries. The symbol of Aries is a ram. I
remembered seeing scores of ram-headed sphinxes in Egypt. In
the trance, I was shown that in the age of Aries, power was concen-
trated in a single individual. The focus was on the leader, and the
rest of the population was content to serve in subordinate roles.

The age of Pisces introduced the idea of duality. Two fish,
swimming in opposite directions, opposed to each other. A voice
spoke to me, saying that in this age humans learned to play two
destructive games: the "I'm right–you're wrong" game and the
equivalent "I win–you lose" game. Society took sides. It was the
age of egos. It gave us the inquisition, undermined the status of
women, and created the environment that allowed Spanish con-
quistadores to demolish the ancient cultures of Central and South
America in the name of Christianity. This, I was told, is the reason
for so much confrontation in our world.

Instead of one powerful individual, more people rose to posi-
tions of power and wealth in the age of Pisces. Now, as we transition to the age of Aquarius, people are beginning to ask questions
about the social order. I remember being a student during the Viet-
nam war. The opposition to that war divided the country. On one
side you had the protesters, and on the other side the "my country
right or wrong" crowd. Questioning the validity of our government was unheard of in the past. Something was changing in our
culture.

As my trance continued, I could see society splintering into
small vocal groups as a consequence of moving into a new world
energy. The "winners" in the age of Pisces are going to hang onto

the past, clinging to it with all their might. On the other side are the people ready to embrace a new way of thinking. We are questioning what we were taught. We are choosing a new path. The people who think they have everything figured out in black and white are feeling threatened, nervous, and reactive. I was told this transformation would take 150 years.

Today, when I witness the name calling, I understand that it is part of the process of changing from one age to another. Consciousness is rising. Following the rules is fading. I wish I could be around to see what will happen in the future. But from what I was shown, it will be a far better age. I never had a chance to share what I learned with my group. But the experience answered the question that had puzzled me for a very long time.

When the week was over, I took Ian into London for two nights, so that he could see some of the city. I had purchased tickets for the musical *Billy Elliot*, composed by Elton John. We took the tube to Victoria Station and picked up our tickets. With two hours to kill before the performance, I suggested that we go to Buckingham Palace. I told Ian that we were in the city of Westminster, which was rather small. Somewhere fairly nearby was the palace. I asked him to take us there.

Ian wanted directions, but I didn't know how to get there. I told him to ask Spirit to take him to the palace—that when he came to a street corner, he should look left, right, or straight ahead and wait for a pull in one direction. He did this, and I followed him. He led us right to Buckingham Palace, even though there were a lot of turns involved in getting there. "Well done, young Skywalker" I said. We had watched Star Wars the night before on television. I wanted Ian to know that Spirit was now part of his life, not just something that happened in his group sessions. It will be interesting to see what he accomplishes in his life.

The training and encouragement I've received at the college has made me a far better medium—and a far better person. The planet is lucky to have a place like this.

I often wrote down quotes from my teachers that touched me. "Where is life going? Driving at night the headlights illuminate only twenty yards ahead, yet you're not afraid. Enjoy the journey."

The last statement in my journal says it all:

"What an amazing and miraculous process this is! What a privilege to witness and do this work."

Chapter 4

How It Works

I'D SAY THE HARDEST THING to accept about mediumship is that it always feels like I'm making the whole thing up. In thinking about it though, I realized that I never know any of these people so how could I ever be sure of the facts? It will *always* feel like I'm making the whole thing up.

Let me give you an example. Let's say that I ask you to make up a short story and write it down. You write about a man named Edward who married a lady named Thelma. Edward was a newspaper editor. Thelma stayed home with her three kids, two boys and a girl.

You finish your story and then read it to a group of people, only to find that somebody in that group actually knows Edward. He did marry a lady named Thelma; they did have three kids, two boys and a girl; and he *was* a newspaper editor. You would be shocked, right? Well, that's exactly how it feels to be a medium. You have to learn to accept that the imaginary story you are telling is, in fact, true

As I mentioned in the preface, I'm an engineer. Engineers like to know and understand how things work. So while I'm in the process of linking with people in the spirit world, I am also trying to analyze how I'm getting that information.

Psychics and Mediums—What's the Difference?

I should start by mentioning that all mediums are psychic, but only a minority of psychics are mediums. So what's the difference? Psychic abilities enable a person to tap into the energy field of another person in order to obtain information. Every person is surrounded by an energy field, which some call an "aura." With the right lighting conditions, I think almost everyone can learn to see at least some of it. The cells in our body, our nervous system, and the neurons in our brain are all using electric signals. Yet the aura is more than just the radiation given off by our life processes. The cocoon of energy enveloping us also contains information. If I tap into a person's energy field, I can find out a lot of things about him or her.

Our energy is also present in the objects we own or wear. I think most people have the ability get information by holding an object, like a ring or watch belonging to someone else, in the left hand. Try it. Hold the object, then simply relax and let images form in your imagination. Believe what you get; most of the time you'll be correct. The technical name for this skill is "psychometry."

I remember being on a cruise ship and admiring the ring worn by the lady sitting next to me. She took it off and let me hold it. Almost instantly I got a mental picture and blurted out, "I see you own a green car." She almost fell off her chair. I can't explain why I got that particular image first. You'll be surprised at how much information you can get this way. Images of where they live, where they work, how many kids they have, and a lot of other details. All this information is coming psychically.

The fact that the items we own are impressed with our energy can be a bad thing. If you've ever sat down on an airplane and suddenly felt sick, it could be that the previous person who sat in that seat was ill. Also you should be aware that when you buy an antique, you are bringing into your home somebody else's energy.

So if you bought an antique lamp and notice that you and your partner are fighting for no reason, it could be that the lamp was owned by people who constantly fought with each other. There is a remedy for this. If the object is small, you can cover it with salt overnight. The salt will absorb whatever energy was present. Obviously, you can't cover a used couch with salt, so the recommended solution is to smudge the couch. Smudging is a practice of taking some herbs and using their smoke to purge the energy of an object—or your whole house for that matter. Smudge sticks are bundles of these herbs tied together, and they are commonly available in any spiritual store or from the web. I use white sage for this purpose. You can do a web search to learn about other alternatives.

It's important for a medium to understand where the information is coming from. If I tell you that I have linked to your father's mother, how do I know that I'm getting that from your grandmother in the spirit world? After all, you know your grandmother, and so some information about her is also stored in your energy field. I think that many people who claim to be mediums are instead getting the information psychically.

There is a way to tell, though. Information coming psychically is very dry and emotionless. It's like reading a shopping list. A gallon of milk, a box of Cheerios, toilet paper, and cream cheese. Isn't that exciting! However, when I link with your grandmother, I start to feel her personality. I may even start to mimic her behavior. If she always scratched her forehead, I may start doing that without even being aware of it. I begin to feel her. Was she a happy gregarious person or a quiet, withdrawn lady. Did she have a loud laugh or a quiet demeanor? How did she view her life? What were her interests? Did she have an easy life or a hard one? How did she feel about dying? Who met her when she crossed over? Who is with her in the spirit world?

A good way to verify that I've got a discarnate spirit rather than a psychic impression is to say something like, "She was the type of woman who …" and then let the spirit fill in the blanks. Once I feel her personality, then I can start probing for specific information.

The most impressive way to prove that the link is not just psychic is to give specific information that the person you're reading does not know. I had a good example of this a couple of summers ago. Ben was spending that summer in South Bend as an intern. Because he didn't know anyone, I had him over for dinner. We were eating outside on the deck, just visiting. I talked about my strange ability to connect to the spirit world. Ben was cautious but open-minded. As we were talking I was interrupted by his paternal grandfather. Among the things he said was that he was with his brother, who had an S name. Ben immediately informed me that his grandfather did not have a brother. Well, in my mind I'm pretty sure that his grandfather knew whether or not he had a brother, so I stuck with what I had said. Ben was absolutely positive that I was wrong.

After Ben went back to his apartment he phoned his father. Sure enough, his grandfather did have a brother with an S name. Due to internal family friction, Ben was never told about him. There's no better proof that the information is coming from a discarnate spirit (a spirit without a body) than when the person you're reading has no knowledge of it.

Many people question mediumship because they assume that when I'm linked to a spirit, it's just like having a conversation with another living person. I wish that were the case. The problem is that spirits vibrate at very high frequencies, while those of us with bodies vibrate at far lower frequencies. The room you are sitting in is full of signals: cellphone signals, television signals, radio signals, and other frequencies that are too high for us to perceive. Just because we can't see them doesn't mean that they don't exist. You may have spirits in your room right now too. It's just that you can't see them.

The diagram below illustrates the link between a medium and a spirit.

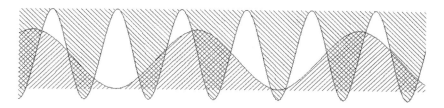

The closely spaced waves on top represent the spirit world, vibrating at high frequencies. The wider waves on the bottom represent living people. Only when the two vibrations overlap does information pass from spirit to the medium. So the information comes in bits and pieces, shown as cross-hatched areas in the diagram. It's the job of the medium to paste the bits together. It's always a challenge.

If you read any books about mediumship, you'll find a list of the classical categories by which the information comes:

- Clairvoyance: seeing things
- Clairaudience: hearing things
- Clairsentience: feeling things

The 3 C's have been around for a long time. However mediumship, like everything else in the universe, is evolving. So now there is a fourth C that has appeared more recently and has been given the name:

- Claircognizance: knowing things

Some Examples

To illustrate how these things work in practice, I'll start by telling you about two readings that I gave at Sacred Waters. Two or three times a year I give what we call a public demonstration. These are open to anyone who wants to come. The goal is to open people's minds and to provide evidence that consciousness survives physical death.

I always begin with a short explanation of the process. However, I had barely started speaking when I saw two feet descending through the high ceiling. I watched with awe and amusement as a man floated down into the room on a parachute!

I told the group what was happening. I thought it was very funny. I said that we must have a paratrooper or a skydiver here. I decided that he was a paratrooper, and I felt that this went back to World War II. I began seeking more information from this man. I learned that he used to like to dance. So I said that this man was talking about his dancing.

At that point a lady in the rear of the room (who I found out later had been dragged there kicking and screaming by a friend of hers) sort of curled up in her chair and acknowledged that it was her husband. I told her that her husband wanted to acknowledge a special event like a birthday or anniversary that was happening around that time. She replied that the next day was their anniversary. I summed it up by telling her, "Well, your husband has just parachuted into the room to wish you a happy anniversary!"

Right after the paratrooper left I looked to my right and started laughing. I was seeing a dog wearing pants! I blurted out, "Somebody had a dog with a clothing name." After I said that, I saw the questioning looks in the room, and then thought to myself what a stupid thing to say. I could not imagine a clothing name for a dog. But a lady raised her hand, and said that she had a dog named Levi Jones. Now everybody understood the pants. Levi was now with her father in the spirit world, so that led to a link with her father.

The lady whose husband came by parachute was obviously shaken up by what had happened. So after the session ended I went over to her and asked if she was okay. I don't want anyone leaving who still has questions or feels uncomfortable. She told me that she had conspired with the funeral director to put her husband's paratrooper boots in the coffin with him before they sealed it, and her husband was known for his dancing, so she knew right away that it had to be him.

When you have a group of thirty or forty people, I think the spirits are challenged to find a way to single out the one person in the group that they want to reach. I never fail to admire the clever ways they find to do that. The parachute and the pants were brilliant ideas on their part. In that way there was no doubt about which person they wanted to reach.

Now that I've given you a description of what happened, I'd like to review exactly how I got that information. In this way you can better understand the process.

Clairvoyance

I started by saying that I saw some feet coming through the ceiling, followed by legs, then the whole person, and then the parachute. Part of the problem in explaining what actually happened is that we humans only have words for our five senses. If the man were solid, then everyone in the room would have seen him. So what does it mean to say that I "saw" him?

The truth is that I did not see him with my eyes. Yet I absolutely, positively knew that this was happening. It made me laugh; it amazed me. Some part of me was aware of what was happening, but that information was not coming from my eyes. I have come to believe that it is my unconscious mind that is seeing the invisible. My subconscious mind then either creates an image in my imagination or just a sense of "knowing" to tell my conscious mind what it is perceiving.

If I see this in my imagination, then the information is coming clairvoyantly.

Try this exercise. See if you can imagine a blackboard in front of you. Draw a circle on the blackboard. Can you see that? Then erase the circle and draw a square. Can you see that in your imagination? If so, welcome to clairvoyance. It never gets any better than that. John Edward, the well-known and respected medium previously mentioned, calls it "cloudy-voyance," which better fits the actual experience. Most of us can see things in our imagination, or mind screen. The spirit who wishes to link with us will project the images. Often these are very quick and fleeting, so part of the process is to be hyper-aware of what we are thinking about. In a sense, mediums become detached observers of what's going on in their own minds and imaginations.

Clairvoyance can also refer to seeing things that are outside our own heads. This is rarer, but it happens. In this case the spirit projects an image into the space around us. It requires a lot more effort for them to achieve this.

When I describe the person I'm seeing clairvoyantly, it's the spirit's way of identifying himself or herself. In the world of spirit there are no physical bodies. For example, in another public demonstration I saw a man in a wheelchair. From the way the blanket on his lap sagged, I could tell that he had lost his left leg. The man turned out to be a friend's father. I was really surprised because we had never discussed her father before.

When this man crossed over, his health and his leg were restored. Or that is our concept of it, since in fact he no longer has a body. So if he is now in perfect condition, why did he project an image of himself in a wheelchair? Obviously, if he had come in any other way, his daughter might not recognize him. So the spirit will project an image that the sitter will recognize. But when you picture your loved ones in the spirit world, think of them as the happiest and healthiest they have ever been, because that's how they are now.

The paratrooper gave me an image of dancing shoes. This is shorthand notation for me. Over many readings, I find the same images flash into my imagination when describing a particular thing. The symbols make it much easier to get information. Boxes mean somebody is moving or just moved. A typewriter means that the person is writing something. The spirit world can draw on my library of symbols to aid in communicating with me. Names work the same way. If I see a flash image of my great aunt, I know that the name "Rose" is somehow connected to the spirit or the family I'm working with. It speeds up communication. The technical term for this is symbology.

Clairsentience

I mentioned earlier that because the man was using a parachute, he had to be either a paratrooper or a skydiver. I could tell which was correct because I got some feedback from the spirit. It's hard to describe this, but I can give you an idea of what it feels like. Sometimes you have to search for a name in your memory, but you keep drawing a blank. We all know that feeling. Then suddenly the name comes to you, and you feel an emotional reaction. It's a feeling of satisfaction, accomplishment, or relief that you finally remembered that name. I get that kind of feeling when I'm thinking of the correct choice. I use this often. Is it her father's mother or her mother's mother? I'll get an internal reaction when I've thought of the correct option.

I told the lady that her husband wanted to acknowledge a special occasion happening around that time. This came from a feeling rather than an image. It felt like I was anticipating a party of some kind. That's a hard feeling to describe, but over many readings it has become very familiar to me. Since it's a feeling, it is coming clairsentiently.

While it didn't happen in this case, if I had more time to link with this man, I would have asked him how he passed away. If I get pain in my chest, it would indicate a heart attack. If I get that pain and also a blackness in my imagination, I would say he had lung cancer. If my legs feel weak, I would say he had trouble walking. All that information is coming from feelings within my own body. This is clairsentience.

Clairsentience is the fundamental skill of mediumship. If I cannot feel the person I'm perceiving, the way they thought, the way they behaved, their attitude towards their life, then I haven't got a true link with them. If you subtract this skill, then all I'll have is information coming psychically from the energy field of the sitter. That is not mediumship.

Altered States

I brought up Levi Jones, the dog wearing pants, because it illustrates a couple of things. As soon as I perceived this (in my imagination), I blurted out the statement, "Someone had a dog with a clothing name." Had I thought about it, I never would have said that because I couldn't think of a clothing name that would fit a dog. If I stop to analyze something, the link is broken immediately. So I have learned to just open my mouth and let the words come out, unplanned and unedited. Often I'm really surprised by what I just said, as in this case. It's my voice, but it didn't come from my logical mind.

This is a special state of being. At the Arthur Findlay College they call this "stepping into the power." Others call it an "altered state." Basically, you check your logical mind at the door and then freely give whatever comes to you. This lets the spirit talk through you, in a manner of speaking. It is not a trance state, just a relaxed state with all the internal editing controls disabled. You might have guessed that as an engineer, this was the hardest thing for me to do. It also means that I forget most of what I say at a reading. People will come up to me later and say that they checked on a fact that I had reported, and I was correct. I thank them, but I really can't remember anything about that reading.

Sometimes I get names. Names are hard to get, at least some

of the time. I describe it as trying to hear a faint voice on the radio with lots of static. Then at other times names are almost shouted at me. If I am hearing something, then I'm using the skill of clairaudience. This skill works in two ways. The most common way is to hear something in my own voice. The other way is to hear something in the spirit's voice. But that has only happened to me once, and it surprised me so much that I couldn't even remember what she said. More commonly I see letters forming above someone's head. The letter S formed near Ben when his grandfather was talking about his brother. So in that case I got the letter through clairvoyance.

Claircognizance

At this level of my evolution, the skill I seem to be using the most is the new one, claircognizance. I just *know* things, without any rational way of knowing. I don't have to wait for symbols or pictures or feelings, I just know. Perhaps one explanation for this is that mediumship has evolved. If you read the literature of the last century, you will find descriptions of a spirit guide sitting on the lap of the medium and relaying information. Also in the last century, many people were trained for physical mediumship—the manipulation of physical objects. Tables rattled and cardboard megaphones flew around the room. Today people are busy and can't train for years to do these things. We accept the existence of the spirit world, and they don't have to rattle a table to convince us. So it makes sense to bypass the physical phenomena altogether and have a mind-to-mind link.

So I may use words like, "Your brother is telling me about the time you stepped on a wasp nest," but what's really happening is that I just *know* that this happened, and not that I'm receiving verbal dictation from your brother. This also pops up spontaneously. At another public demonstration, I was working with a lady in the middle of the room and happened to glance at a lady on my left.

Without any thought I just blurted out, "You have a sister in spirit who was a florist." Goodness! Where did that come from? It was not a conscious choice to say that. Actually, the entire night was rather strange. The first lady's sister was involved with the mafia. My first clue was that I saw a body in the trunk of a black Lincoln. The second lady's sister supplied flowers to the mafia. They did not know each other at all. We jokingly called it, "Mafia Night at Sacred Waters."

If you get a reading from a medium, pay attention to the language being used. This can provide insight into how the information is being received. The most amazing reading I've ever received was from Colin Bates, a tutor at the Arthur Findlay College. At one point he said, "As I'm starting to feel the smile and the energy, and there is a terrific smile here, and you have photographs of the smile. You have photographs of the face and the head and this tremendous smile …" What struck me is that he didn't say that he *saw* the smile, he said that he *felt* the smile. If you hear something like this, you know immediately that he was getting this through clairsentience. Pay attention to the choice of words, and you will begin to be able to sort out how the information is coming through.

Predicting the Future

The last thing I want to discuss is what the limitations are for this kind of work. We've all seen ads telling you to consult a self-proclaimed psychic with a name like Madame Lipochinsky to learn your future. Save your money. Nobody can predict the future. If you had married Sam instead of Edgar, you would have a different future. If you had gone to Yale instead of Harvard, you would have a different future. At this very moment you are creating your own future.

I'll discuss reincarnation in a later chapter. But for now imagine that before you are born into this world, you decide what obstacles to confront and overcome in the process of perfecting your soul. In a way, you cannot escape those events because you agreed to them ahead of time. If you quit the game through suicide, you'll have to come back again and face the same obstacles. So in that way at least part of the future is inevitable. But no psychic can tell you that you'll meet a rich person and spend your life on a yacht. That's crazy. I do sometimes get information like, "I see you're going on a cruise to Alaska," but I'm saying that because it's already in your plans and therefore in your energy field.

Unexpected Spirits

I want you to understand that a medium is a kind of radio receiver. I cannot summon anyone, for the same reason that you can't look at a radio playing a song by Sting and ask it to play "Beethoven's Ninth." But like a radio, I can turn myself off. Or at least try.

Although I shut off the spirit world when I'm not working as a medium, occasionally a spirit needs to come through and will break through all my barriers. An example occurred one morning in my synagogue. They had put the Torah scroll back in the ark, and we were singing the ancient melody used for that ceremony. I was totally engrossed in singing, when I saw a woman standing next to a congregant who was standing in front of the ark. She told me to tell him not to forget her birthday. Now this presented a problem. The man is a college professor, and I had no idea what he would think of spirits in general, let alone one standing next to him. I thought about it for a while and decided that I needed to honor this lady, who must have worked very hard to break through for a good reason. I approached the professor and told him that I had no idea what he'd make of this, but that I had seen a lady standing next to him, and she had tremendous love for him, and she didn't want him to forget her birthday. He got very emotional and had tears in his eyes. His mother's birthday was the next day. I'm glad I had the courage to approach him. My philosophy is that I work for the spirit world and not for the person in front of me. So when in doubt, I choose to honor the spirit regardless of what the reaction is. I am not here to sell anything to anyone. I am here to serve as a voice for the people in the world of spirit.

Sometimes I think spirits come through just because I'm there and I can sense them. It can be confusing sometimes. I had a sitting in Michigan with five members of a single family. The husband of one of the ladies had the most to say. Then I saw a man standing in the corner of the room. He was holding a rifle, and there were rabbits at his feet. I understood that he was a hunter and used to hunt rabbits. The family in the room was appalled. They opposed all forms of hunting. As I always do in this situation, I tried getting more information from the spirit. But the family could not relate at all to anything I said. At that point I felt another man come in. He was the husband and father of the ladies in the group. I worried that my credibility had been shattered by the hunter episode.

After the group had gone, Marj, whose facility had been used for the meeting, came in and sat down. I told her about how this hunter had come in and nobody could relate to him. She knew immediately who it was. The man had lived in a house behind hers, in the exact direction in which I had seen him. Marj's husband had done a favor for the man once, and he came to their home with rabbit meat as a thank you. He had passed away a few years before. All the information I had was true. I asked Marj if she would be kind enough to tell the previous group that I was not completely crazy after all.

At other times, spirits may come through because you know the people they are trying to reach. In this case, you are being asked to serve as the medium to pass on the information. A typical example happened at my first public demonstration at Sacred Waters. It sometimes happens that as I'm driving there, a couple of spirits make their presence known. They are trying to beat the crowd, I think. On this particular night three spirits got my attention while I was driving.

The first two spirits were instantly recognized by people in the audience. But nobody could identify the third. This was a young boy sitting on his grandmother's lap. He had brown eyes and dark hair—and looked to be about five years old. The loss of a child is so traumatic that anyone in the room who had experienced this would immediately react. But as much as I tried, no one acknowledged the little boy and his grandmother. Finally I had to move on.

At the end of the session I was really tired and sat down. It still bothered me that we had never identified the little boy. In my mind I said, "Okay, Grandma, you've got one more shot at this." Then I heard the word "co-worker." So I told the group that this boy belonged to a co-worker. Instantly, a lady knew who I was talking about. It was indeed the son of a lady she worked with. The beautiful part of this reading was that her co-worker's mother had died just a couple of weeks before. So the message was that she was now united with her grandson in the spirit world, and he was sitting on her lap. What a beautiful message! The lady in my group said that she would definitely pass this message on to her co-worker, who I'm sure appreciated the news that her son and her mother were together now.

There is a story in the Bible's First Book of Samuel that tells a tale about the witch of Endor. The prophet Samuel had died, and King Saul wanted advice from him. So he sought out a witch, or medium to use the modern vernacular, and asked her to summon the spirit of Samuel. The spirit of Samuel was very angry over being awakened, and cursed the king saying that his army will fall to the Philistines. That's exactly what happened, and Saul committed suicide.

This passage has sometimes been used to condemn the type of work that I and other mediums do. However, I have a big problem with the story. How can I summon someone? How can I force them to come through? Can I threaten them? They're already dead! Can

I put a gun to their head? They don't have a head! So the idea that a medium can force someone to come through is silly. Therefore if you come to me wanting to hear from your mother, and you get Great Aunt Sally, please accept and love Great Aunt Sally. You can and should ask the people you want to hear from to please show up, but if they don't, I can't change that. It doesn't mean they don't love you.

I have often wondered why the first person to come through in a private reading can be someone rather remote. You wanted your father, and you get your third cousin's second husband's mother, or a classmate from grade school that you haven't thought about in decades. It happens often enough that I have formed a theory about it. Like all forms of energy, I vibrate at a certain frequency. I think that some spirits find it easier to blend their energies with mine. They try me on, like trying on an overcoat, and see if I fit. Once this initial blending occurs, then they can act to help bring through the people you really want to hear from. If you don't recognize the first person who comes through, think of someone you know who may be a distant relative or friend. They are just trying to help forge the link with me.

Also, please don't reject the person who does come through. Several times, I've brought through someone who gets a nasty response. "I don't want to talk to her!" Listen to what this spirit has to say, even if it was a horrible relationship. Remember, the whole process is powered by love. If you're that angry with someone, it means you are tied to them energetically. It's a short circuit, and it isn't doing you any good to spend your vital energy resenting or hating someone. Give them a chance to apologize. Love them if you can. We are all struggling to make ourselves better souls, including those people who gave us a hard time.

BOOK THREE

What I Learned Along the Way

Chapter 5

Losing a child

"YOU HAVE A DAUGHTER IN SPIRIT who was brutally murdered," I said in the calmest voice I could muster. The video in my head kept playing, and I watched in horror as this beautiful young lady was being butchered alive by a crazed killer. I struggled to maintain my composure as her mother sobbed softly.

Sadly, a large number of people who come for a sitting have lost a child. I can see the grief in their eyes and the sadness that permeates their energy field. I have great compassion for them. My mother lost a child too. My sister Diane, who was closest to me in age, died from liver cancer at the age of forty-six. My sister Maribeth lost her only child. Her son was only thirty-two. So that kind of loss has touched my family too.

What impresses me is how the children try to comfort their parents.

The young victim of the brutal knife attack is a good example. The first thing she wanted her mother to know was that she didn't suffer. She had blacked out almost immediately at the beginning of the attack. Then I continued, "Your daughter is talking about being a cheerleader."

"My daughter hated sports, and was never a cheerleader," her mother insisted.

In cases like this one, I always choose to go with what I'm getting. "Well, your daughter says she was a cheerleader." Then I described the building and the circumstances, and her mother finally remembered the occasion. Her daughter was really young at the time, and the incident was very funny.

Then her daughter told me about a train trip they had taken.

Mom denied it. I insisted that they had taken the South Shore train together to Chicago. Then she remembered it, and there was another humorous incident associated with the trip. This went on for about an hour—one story after another about the times they had together and the funny things that happened to them.

As the session came to a close, I looked at this dear lady and said, "When you think of your daughter, all you can think of is how she died. Your daughter just spent an hour reminding you of how she lived. That's how she wants you to remember her." I heard from some of her friends afterwards that the session had truly changed her and that she was feeling much more positive.

Dealing with the murder of a child has to be a horrific experience for any parent. But in my work I've come to believe that suicide is even worse. It leaves the parents wondering what they could have done differently, what signals they missed, and on and on. This may haunt them for years.

I've linked with several suicides. The first thing I have noticed is that there appears to be no condemnation associated with it. My Catholic upbringing insisted that any suicide would face an eternity in hell. This isn't true. Some suicides have brain chemistry problems and are not held responsible. Others chose to end their lives to avoid a long and painful death. They seem to be doing well in the spirit world.

The penalty for suicides, especially those who took their lives as a form of revenge (I'll make you sorry), is that they now have to feel the pain that their suicide caused their families and friends. They are the ones who come to apologize for their behavior—and for the pain they caused.

Sometimes a person will come through to explain why they took their own lives. I had a recent example of this. This lady's son had shot himself in the face with a shotgun. She didn't understand what drove him to do this. Her son explained that he had fallen in love with a girl—and that girl's family had rejected him and forbade him from seeing her again. He fell into a deep depression and took his own life. At least now his mother understands what happened. It is a very sad thing for any young person to end his life. This young man now feels the pain that his suicide caused his family and friends.

Those who commit suicide to escape an unpleasant or embarrassing situation are making a bad mistake. Their souls cannot evolve to a higher level until they return to earth and successfully face the same kind of situation. There is no running away from the challenge that we agreed to face before our incarnation into this world.

What I try to do to help parents grieving the loss of a child is to find out who met their child when the child arrived in the spirit world. I also want to know if there's someone in the spirit world watching out for them.

A couple from Arizona came with some family members for a group session. I heard a name like "Kirsten," but they told me the name was "Carston." When I first get a name, I don't really know much about the person. If the spirit gives me an ambiguous name, I might not be able to tell whether I'm linked to a boy or a girl at first. I try to push my sensitivity out to them and embrace them so that they know I care about them. In this case, I immediately got the feeling that Carston was a small boy. I wanted to know how he ended up on the other side. Carston just said, "I couldn't breathe." I found out after the session that he had drowned in his parent's swimming pool. I cannot imagine how much his parents were blaming themselves and how horrible that would be. I asked Carston who he was with. He told me that he was with his aunt. I wanted to know if she was his father's sister or his mother's sister. It was his mother's sister. I asked his aunt how she arrived on the other side. She said that she had died from cancer several years before. I was able to tell his parents that he's fine, that he's with his mother's sister, who had died from cancer several years before.

Just knowing this lifted a huge weight off them.

At times like this I want to learn more about the spirit world. Carston showed himself playing with his dog. Then he told me that he was going to school. He liked the fact that he could bring his dog with him to school. I asked him to show me his school. I had a vision of this large transparent structure, which looked like an assembly of vertical crystals. I had seen this image once before when I linked to a young child. I asked what he was studying, but Carston didn't answer.

His parents wanted to know if Carston's aunt was taking care of him. I got an interesting answer to this question. She told me that she is aware of him but that in this place he doesn't need watching, because there is no danger here—it's like having a million mothers looking out for him. I found that very comforting. He had already made many friends, and most of the time he was with his friends.

Knowing this will not bring him back to be with his parents. But now they know that he's fine, that his aunt is there with him, that he has many friends and his dog, and that he's going to school. I hope it really helped lessen their grief a bit.

Some children pass from accidents like Carston's, and others pass from diseases. When I link with a child who passed from a disease, I almost always get the feeling that in some way the child knew ahead of time that they would pass. Sometimes they write things that their parents find later. Sometimes it's just the way their child behaves—with maturity far beyond their years. I've had children who saw angelic beings around them while they were alive and told their parents about them.

Again, these children primarily want to comfort their parents. They will acknowledge the love of their parents. If they had siblings, they will give me names or specific items belonging to a sister or brother, as a way of bringing them into the conversation. I've also found that many times a surviving sibling will have experienced a visit from their spirit brother or sister. In this case, the spirit child wants the sibling to know that the visit was real.

Children can also send signs to their parents. Two of the most popular items are pennies and butterflies. I've had parents report a huge swarm of butterflies outside their windows. My favorite penny story came during a public demonstration at Sacred Waters.

I saw a male spirit standing in the aisle between two people in the audience—a man seated on his left and a woman to his right. He gave me the relationship of "brother." It turned out he was the brother of the lady and had passed from a heart attack. While I was probing him for more evidence, I suddenly saw a grilled cheese sandwich. In fact, I saw three of them, cut into triangles, sitting on a little plate. It was totally incongruous with the brother's story. I just looked her straight in the eye and said simply, "grilled cheese sandwiches." She burst into tears.

She had lost a young son from a brain tumor. Apparently he was actually born with it, but nobody knew about it. His favorite food was grilled cheese sandwiches, and she always made three of them. The link with her son was profound. Normally, I try to stay completely detached so that I can be objective. It isn't easy. I confess that I'm normally a hopeless romantic who gets teary eyed when two people hug on TV. No matter how hard I tried in this case, I couldn't help being drawn to her son. He was a being of such pure light, of such pure love, that I couldn't help myself.

He was one of those enlightened beings that Buddhists call a bodhisattva. These spirits come to earth to be teachers. They create situations in which many people can learn and grow just by knowing them. This young boy had affected many, many lives in the short time he was on the earth. Yet it was the purity of his light that entranced me.

Her son told me to tell his mother that he had sent her pennies. She couldn't believe that I had just said that. One morning she had gotten up, and next to a photo of him was a pile of pennies! She had no idea whatsoever where they could have come from. I've heard similar stories from other people who have lost a loved one.

I will never forget what his soul felt like. It was the first time ever that I had to take a short break because I was being overwhelmed by what I was seeing and feeling.

Other children who have come through were rebels in some way. They may have died in an accident while driving drunk, from a drug overdose, or even from being shot by the police. I had a case like that during a public demonstration. Both his parents were there. He said that he fell in with a group who valued breaking the rules above all else. They had something like a contest to see who could do the most outrageous things. He had alcohol problems. He had drug problems. He was defiant towards his parents and would purposely do things that aggravated them.

That evening he came through to apologize for his behavior. "I now understand that everything you did, and everything you said, was motivated out of love for me. You were wonderful parents. I'm sorry I was such a lousy kid."

It must be terrible to try your best to raise a child with good values, only to have that child defy you and do things that you know will harm them. Yet each child has free will, and so parents have only limited power over their children. I am always pleased when a child like this comes through to let his parents know that they appreciate their parents, knowing that they did the best they could, and that the child now understands that his parents always wanted the best for him.

I've often wished that there was an *Encyclopedia of the Spirit World,* so that I could go look up answers to the many questions that I have about that world. But no such document exists. Instead, in doing many readings I have learned quite a bit about the spirit world, and occasionally something comes up that answers one of my questions.

For example, I had always wondered what happens to those children who do not make it into the physical world. One day I got my answer.

A lady drove several hours to have a private sitting with me. She was obviously pregnant. The first person who made her presence known was a lady named Mary. My sitter said that she did not know anyone named Mary. As I always do, I asked Mary for more information. She told me that she had changed this lady's diapers when she was a baby, and also those of her brother. Mary had helped to raise her.

Suddenly there was the light of recognition. I understood that her mother had died when she was a baby, but I never learned exactly what relationship Mary had to her. While I'm always curious to know things like that, I can't stop and ask questions. As long as my sitter understands, it's good enough for me. The point was that Mary had taken care of her and her brother when she was a baby.

Next came something totally unexpected. Mary told me that my sitter had two miscarriages. The first was a girl and the second was a boy. The lady did not know the sex of the first child she lost, but she did know that the second child was a boy. Ultrasound had shown that he was terribly deformed and would not survive, so they chose to terminate the pregnancy. Then Mary told me that she was raising this lady's unborn children on the other side! Wow!

You can imagine what their mother's reaction was to that news. The very lady who had taken care of her as an infant was now doing the same thing for her unborn children. It was one of those moments that infused me with such joy and such love for the spirit world. Now I know that children who don't make it into this world still have a life on the other side. It is such a beautiful concept.

Parents who have lost a child who was physically or mentally challenged want to know whether their child is able to get along on the other side. The answer is that these disabilities vanish when the child crosses over. Once again, I find that these children are usually advanced souls who volunteer to accept their limited abilities and be born into this world to teach love and compassion. They may be low-functioning in our world, but on the spiritual level they are often the most advanced.

All children who pass at an early age will try and give some evidence of survival to their loved ones. So pay attention to unusual things around you, and when your child comes to you in a dream, the probability is that the visit is real.

As I told the mother whose son passed from a brain tumor, every time you find a penny, think of it as a hug and a kiss from your son. Because that's what it is.

Chapter 6

Animals in the Spirit World

IT WAS THE END OF MY FIRST WEEK at the Arthur Findlay College. I was in the beginner's group. Sue Taylor was my tutor. We had spent the first several days doing various experiments designed to help us discover our abilities, including attempts to link with discarnate spirits for our partners.

As I've discussed, there is a big difference between getting information psychically and getting information from a discarnate spirit. The courses at the Arthur Findlay College had some exercises intended to help us distinguish the difference. Toward the end of my first week there, our tutor Sue asked us to stand up and attempt to link with someone in the spirit world for a member of our group. Up until that point, we had been working with one person at a time. She asked me to go first. I took a deep breath, and just let my imagination run wild. The first thing I saw was a goat, a black-and-white goat. Now, this is not what I was expecting. Nor was it what Sue was expecting. In fact, she gave me a disapproving frown.

Meanwhile, the goat led me down a gravel path past a chicken coop.

At that point I think Sue was ready to make me sit down. "Get on with it," she scowled.

The goat then led me to a two-story white farmhouse. There was a water pump in the back yard. There was a fence across the road with horses beyond it. There was a large tree to the right of a driveway with a tire swing on it.

The goat turned out to be the childhood pet of a lady in the class. I ended up bringing through three generations of her family who had lived in that house. As it turned out, the first thing I was able to link with on the other side was a goat. Thank you, Mr. Goat!

Since then I've done many readings where animals show up. One of the most memorable was a one-on-one session with a tall, very masculine man. He had a crew cut—and seemed to be all business. The first thing I got was an image of him standing next to a tank—a military tank, not a water tank. I told him what I saw, and he just nodded yes. Then I got the name Robbie. He understood that. I told him that Robbie and he were best friends. They competed in some kind of sport where they traveled together to hold the competitions. He calmly said yes to all this. Robbie had died suddenly. I even got the name of the street he lived on. This man showed absolutely no emotion at all. I mean, this was his best friend who had died suddenly. The information coming from Robbie was right on the nose. No reaction, no emotion whatever. When the half-hour reading was over, we stood up and at that moment I got another image. I blurted out, "You had a German shepherd." His eyes opened wide. I can't remember the dog's name, so we'll call him Fido. Then I got another impression and said to him, "Robbie wants you to know that he's got Fido on the other side waiting for you." The man broke into tears. It was the dog who finally got to him.

I remember another incident involving a dog. We had broken up into pairs as usual to exchange readings. My partner and I pulled our chairs a little distance from a neighboring pair to get some privacy. I started to read my partner, when I was distracted by the spirit of a collie. The poor collie was sitting at the foot of a lady in the next pair and madly wagging its tail. The dog shifted its weight from foot to foot, shuffled a little bit, and looked really anxious. I could not concentrate at all on my partner because I was so distracted by this dog trying to get her master's attention. Finally, I'd had enough. I got up out of my chair, walked over to this lady, and said rather bluntly, "For goodness sakes, please acknowledge your collie. She's been trying for several minutes to get your attention, and it's making me crazy!" The lady was thrilled that her collie came to her. The collie was happy. I went back to my reading.

I've also gotten quite a few horses. At my last visit to the college, we were having a service in the Sanctuary. Right down the middle of the aisle came a man riding a horse! The next day I asked my tutor if he had seen the horse and rider. He hadn't. But later that day we were asked to pair up again, and I asked the lady who was my partner if she knew a man who rode horses. I knew that he had two brothers and some other specific facts about him. She knew exactly who I was talking about. I was happy to place the horse and rider with the right person. When I see something like that, I feel an obligation to find the person the spirit wants to reach, and I was really happy to do that in this case.

I also got a rabbit once, while doing a private sitting back home. I saw this little furry critter, and at first I thought it was a cat. I told the lady what I was seeing; she said that it wasn't a cat, it was a rabbit. Well, this animal definitely didn't have the upright ears that I associate with rabbits. It turned out that her beloved pet rabbit had floppy ears. So I learned something new.

By far the most numerous animals that come through are dogs. Followed by horses, then cats. Just one goat and a rabbit so far.

Well, I did get an elephant once. A huge, full size elephant! It happened during a public demonstration at Sacred Waters. The elephant was standing next to Joyce, the lady who runs the facility. It was gigantic, with colored paint on its forehead, and a garland of flowers around its neck. Now if ever there was a test about trusting what you get, this would be it. It turns out that Joyce is very interested in Hinduism, and so the elephant meant something to her after all. I've often wondered whether the other people who came that night thought I was crazy. Joyce attracts some interesting animals. At the next public demonstration, I saw a cobra sitting at the entrance to a cave right behind her. Before I said anything, I pleaded with Joyce not to freak out and told her that there was this cobra sitting at the entrance to a cave right behind her. It turned out that this was a sacred symbol for the Hindu saint, Gauri Ma, for whom the hall we were sitting in was named. Joyce was happy, and I was relieved.

You may recall the couple from Arizona who had lost their young son, Carston, in a drowning accident. Carston showed himself playing with his dog. I found out that the dog had passed away shortly after the boy died. I've often thought that the dog wanted to cross over to be company for his young friend. Animals are wonderful and have deep compassion for us.

I don't think that every animal has a unique spirit that crosses over. Rather, I think that wild animals share what I would call a group consciousness. It's like a shared awareness. Flocks of birds and schools of fish seem to turn all at once. Perhaps that's evidence of a shared consciousness.

On the other hand, animals who live in close relationships with humans seem to develop a consciousness apart from their group. It's these animals who make it to the other side, retaining their bonds with their human friends. While I've seen dozens of animals on the other side, each of which was attached to a human, I've never seen a group of wild animals.

The lesson? Know that your animal friends are waiting for you on the other side. Love—both your love for an animal and the love of an animal for you—never dies.

Chapter 7

Facing Alzheimer's Disease

MY MOTHER HAS DEMENTIA of the Alzheimer's type, which is the official clinical diagnosis. It has been painful to watch her drift away slowly but inexorably.

Mom was one of eight kids born in the Depression to a Catholic working-class family. Her ambition was to rise above her humble beginnings. Pat McKenna had said that in a previous lifetime Mom had been high-born into a patrician family. In this lifetime, Mom moved out of her crowded childhood home to go live with a wealthy family at the invitation of a friend who was an only child. While this is not proof that Pat had been correct, it would explain my mother's search for a more affluent lifestyle. Her leaving home was a blow to her mother and the rest of her family. As an adult she went to beauty parlors, dyed her hair, and liked nice clothes. She had a terrific sense of fun and danced the hula in a small performance group. True to her Germanic background, Mom was always right, and you dared not cross her because you'd be reminded of your infraction until the end of time. Mom was also very conscious of appearances. We were never allowed to sit on the couches in the living room. Those were only for company.

Mom was my defender, but we were never very close. For that matter, my parents were never really close to each other either. Dad would put me down, and then Mom would defend me. I became part of the constant tension between them.

I finally talked to Mom about these things only a few years ago after my father died. She explained that she had her hands full with two babies in diapers and that she basically ignored me because I never caused any trouble. I told Mom that it felt like Dad had never liked me when I was a kid and that I had been afraid of him. From my perspective, Dad had wanted a kid who could be the athlete he aspired to be, and I could not fill that role. She insisted that Dad had always loved me. Then she told me something that shed light on our family relationships. Once she came home and saw Dad slamming my head into the wall repeatedly. "I told him if he ever touched you again I'd bash his brains out with his damned baseball bat." Fortunately, I don't remember that incident.

But I do remember hitting my father. I was a teenager, and I was tired of being treated badly by him. It was a real fight. We even broke some furniture. Mom stepped in to break us up. I'm grateful that Mom would defend me. Yet whenever I tried to hug her, she would pull away. I'm a very touchy-feely kind of person. Mom was not, but she's still my mother.

My relationship with both Mom and Dad improved after Voyager became the first airplane to circle the earth on a single tank of gas. I made the news because I had designed the wings and propellers for that airplane. Then I became a bragging point.

Mom has always been independent. When I was in college she would leave home shortly after Christmas and go to Florida, staying until spring. I looked after my youngest sister when Mom was gone because Dad spent most of his free time hanging out with his buddies at the local country club.

After Dad retired, my parents sold their house in Indiana and bought a house on a golf course in Lehigh Acres, Florida, which became their full-time residence. After Dad died, I'd fly down to visit Mom at least once a year, and she would come back to Indiana for the Christmas holidays and stay with my sister.

The Signs of Alzheimer's

Mom had always been a neat freak. Appearances mattered more than substance. That's why we were never allowed to sit on the couches in the living room. God forbid, there should be a wrinkle on them if company came over. So when I saw her dirty, stained house-dress, I knew that something was wrong. Over time it got worse. When I went to see her, I would find her refrigerator full of moldy food and dirty clothes thrown on the floor in her bedroom.

What worried me the most is whether she could continue to drive. She was very familiar with the small town of Lehigh Acres, but sometimes she would drive over to Fort Myers. I always made her pick me up at the airport and drive back through the busiest streets of Fort Myers, just to see if she knew her way and didn't do anything wrong. Her driving seemed okay for a while.

Still, the situation worsened. We held a family conference and decided it was time to bring her back to Indiana. I'd meet my sisters at various assisted living places at noon, specifically so that we could see the residents and the kind of food they were served. We finally found a place close to my sister Maribeth. The next problem was how to convince my mother to move.

As it turned out, the decision was made for us. We got a phone call from a friend of Mom's who had dropped by her house early in the morning for coffee. Mom was not home, and her car was gone. Her bed had not been slept in. We called the police. I also called the local hospitals to see if she had been admitted. We couldn't find her anywhere. The police even sent out a helicopter to search the swamps in the area.

Meanwhile, about forty miles away, two kids were riding an ATV through some sand dunes near Naples. They saw a car stuck in the sand and went to investigate. My mother was laying down in the sand several yards from the car. They got her up, put her on the ATV, and took her to their house. From there an ambulance took her to the hospital. The hospital would not admit her because there were no actual injuries. They just told her to go home and soak in the bathtub because she had been bitten by sand fleas.

We finally got a friend of hers to drive down and pick her up. After she got home, she did sit in the tub and soak. Now for the second problem. She couldn't get out of the tub! It took a couple more phone calls to get enough people to hoist her out of the bathtub. By this time my sisters and I were ready for a stiff drink.

My niece and her boyfriend were students in Tampa. They drove down and stayed with Mom, and the next day they put her on a plane for home. I explained to the airline that Mom was disoriented, and that she needed to be escorted from one plane to the other in Atlanta, or Lord knows where she'd end up.

I picked her up at the South Bend airport. She was very confused. I told her we had to get her luggage. She said she didn't have any. However, when I took her ticket, I saw that she had two baggage receipts.

In a way this was a blessing. We told Mom that her insurance company had canceled her policy and that the car was totaled. In fact, it took the largest tow truck in the county to pull her car out of the sugar sand. With that objection out of the way, it was easier to convince her to move back north. Maribeth and I flew down to Florida to pack up some of her things. With a lot of effort I was able to clean her car and polish out all the scratches. We sold the bulk of her possessions at auction.

Since then, we've gone through many stages with Mom. First, we had to endure the same question repeated a zillion times. Over time she lost control of her bladder, so she had to wear diapers. Then she had to start using a walker. Then she needed help to eat because she would look at the food and not know what to do with it. Then came silence and a stony, blank expression. We moved her to the memory care unit because she can't do the things that assisted living demands. The doctors say that eventually she will forget how to breathe.

Did I Die?

I've often wondered what's going on in her mind, if anything. I've wondered where her consciousness is. Through the process of giving and receiving readings, I believe that I can now answer that question.

I was giving a platform reading at the Arthur Findlay College to my group when I saw a lady. I described her physical appearance, and got several specific facts connected to her. A man in the audience said, "That's clearly my mother." Then he added the kicker, "But she's still alive." He explained that she had Alzheimer's. I was really surprised. To me she came through like any other person in the spirit world. I turned to Simone, my tutor, because I had no indication that this lady was still living and I was confused. Simone suggested that someone else may be putting out that information and that I should look for this. It did turn out that her husband was also in the spirit world. So I accepted the explanation that her husband was somehow projecting the image and information about his wife.

But something still felt wrong about this. To add to my confusion, during readings from members of my group and also in readings I got from my tutors, my mother would come through. I didn't tell them that she was still living, because I wanted to hear what they had to say. It was definitely my mother. How can that be?

I got my answer later. I was taking my mother to the dentist, back at a time when she was still able to talk. She turned her head and looked at me with a very serious expression, and asked, "Did I die?" What a question! I decided to explore it with her a bit more. Mom is a devout Catholic, so I asked, "Did you go to heaven?"

She replied in a strong voice, "Of course, I went to heaven!" So I asked a key question, "Who met you there?" I know that when we cross over, we are greeted by our loved ones, so I really wanted to hear the answer to that question. Mom went on to name several friends, all of whom were dead.

I have come to believe that advanced Alzheimer's victims in fact are between worlds. They spend part of the time, perhaps most of the time, in the spirit world, and then they have to come back into their debilitated bodies. I've weighed the evidence, both my own experiences with perceiving Alzheimer's victims as spirits and the fact that my classmates and tutors have gotten living Alzheimer's patients as spirits. This has to be the case.

I find it very comforting to know that the shell of the person who used to be my mother is able to visit and adapt to the world of spirit. The Great Spirit is a being of great compassion, and it would be hard to justify making people go through the process of dying an inch at a time without something to comfort them.

Chapter 8

Heaven and Hell

WHEN I WENT to a Catholic school, we were indoctrinated into what they call the catechism. This was their rule book explaining our relationship to God. God was the ultimate judge of our conduct. Follow the rules and we go to heaven. Break the rules and we can spend an eternity in hell. So God's job was to watch our every action and thought—and keep score. There were big sins that would definitely land us in hell, like murdering someone or eating meat on Friday. There were smaller sins that would land us in a place between heaven and hell, called purgatory, for some period of time.

If you wanted to avoid going to hell, then you had to confess your big sins to a priest, who could then absolve you. But as for purgatory, one way to reduce our sentence was to recite short little prayers called, of all things, ejaculations. You can imagine how much fun young Catholic boys had with that term. These ejaculations were phrases like "Jesus, Mary, and Joseph." Each ejaculation reduced your time in purgatory by a specific number of days. Our prayer books gave us the exact number of days that saying each one would subtract from our time in purgatory. How they calculated this was never explained.

The bottom line was that we were constantly being watched and our deeds and misdeeds recorded. Hell and heaven were separate places, with heaven being a place where you were with God in eternal bliss, while hell was a place with eternal punishment and pain.

Well, this turns out to be nonsense. I've linked with more than a hundred people in the spirit world, and over a long period of time I began to understand the truth.

What I've learned is that heaven and hell are states of mind, not specific places. Throughout your life you say and do things that create emotions in other people. If you praise or compliment someone, and give them love and encouragement, it creates in that person an uplifted, happy feeling. If you are mean to people, belittle them, make them feel bad about themselves, you create in them sadness and negative emotions. If you kill someone, then you have also created sadness and grief among their friends and loved ones.

When you cross over to the world of spirit, you are going to feel all the emotions that you created in other people during your lifetime, and those emotions are going to be magnified or multiplied. What you do later in life counts more than the things you did earlier, because we are here to learn and to grow. So if you are a person who is kind and considerate, and makes people happy to be around you, you will experience their happiness magnified. This is heaven.

I recently did a telephone reading for a man in New England. He had lost a daughter and a son. His maternal grandmother and his father also came through to him. Those were loving relationships, and it was a pleasure to communicate that love back to him from the people in the world of spirit. But in the midst of this, I perceived this very dark energy. I told him that this was a person who was very negative, who never smiled, who never had a good thing to say. He said that he did not know anybody like that.

When that kind of thing happens, I go back to the spirit and ask them for more information. The first thing I got was that this was a woman, not a man. He still had no idea who I was talking about. Once again I asked the spirit for more information. I got the impression that this woman was one of his teachers. He thought about it for a bit and then suddenly remembered a nun who was his fourth grade teacher. She had tormented him, belittled him, and made him feel awful. Not only that, she had persuaded his mother to make him repeat the fourth grade, even though he had passed all his subjects. He described her as mean, vindictive, and cruel.

Why would somebody like that want to be brought through to this man? He really did not want to be reminded of that black period in his life. I explained to him that when she crossed over, she suddenly felt the pain that she had created in him and in her other students—and that pain was magnified. This nun was in the hell that she had created, feeling all the pain she had caused.

The man had trouble understanding what I was saying. He had forgiven her a long time ago, he said. I pointed out that she knew that already, but his forgiveness did not relieve her pain— pain that she caused him and pain that she now had to feel. Then I told him something that shocked him. I said that she was now his best friend. That's something that's hard for us to grasp. I explained that the only way to reduce her own pain was for her to do something positive for him. When she does something good for him, then it diminishes the pain she is feeling.

I told him that whenever he needed help with anything, he should ask her. Spirits cannot do everything, but they can put things in our path and help us in other ways. This nun wanted him to know that in a sense she owes him and is ready to help him. That's why she took advantage of my mediumship to connect to this man whose pain she now bears.

It's important that you understand how the system works. You need to know that you will feel the emotions, good or bad, that you have created in your lifetime through your interactions with others. Those emotions will be magnified. This is the true picture of what heaven and hell really are. In fact, you do create your own heaven and your own hell.

My father has come through many times, either through readings with tutors or with classmates, and has always apologized for the way he treated me. At the end of his life we truly loved each other, so he was not asking for forgiveness because none was needed. He just needed to apologize again and again because he now feels the pain he created in me. As a result, when I need something, I always ask Dad, because I know that he'll do whatever he can to help me.

Helping Place

I've often wondered what the people in the spirit world do. Are they just floating around somewhere outside of space and time? I got a clue from one of my classmates at the Arthur Findlay College. Her name was Fiona, and she was from Australia. She was in England while her husband minded her two young daughters.

Fiona told me a story about her youngest daughter. From the time she was able to talk she kept mentioning, "Helping Place." Her parents didn't understand what she was trying to say. One day, when her daughter was a bit older, Fiona asked her what she meant by "Helping Place." Her daughter replied, "That's what we do over there, we help people."

One day Fiona overheard her daughter talking to a cousin who was about the same age. Her daughter was explaining that before she returned to earth, a man who her daughter thought must be Jesus came to her and asked her to pick her mother. The little girl went on to say that she could have chosen Aunt Dorothy or Aunt Rita, "but I picked Mommy."

Out of the mouth of babes, as the expression goes. In the group reading with medium Suzane Northrop, I was told that my sister Diane was helping seeing-eye dogs lead their blind masters. So spirits on the other side apparently spend their time helping people who are still living on earth. They have jobs. The story of picking her mother also made sense to me. I do think we choose our parents and the circumstances of our life before we come back in physical form. We set out the challenges we agree to face—the difficulties we have to overcome.

I think it is a rare thing for a child to remember his or her existence before coming to this world, but there is an old Jewish folk tale that explains why. Before you return to earth, the story goes, the Angel of Forgetfulness comes and presses its finger under your nose and makes you forget your past lives. That's why humans have a dent under our noses.

But as with Fiona's daughter, it happens. My friends Pat and Karen have four children. Their youngest boy always seemed withdrawn and sad. When he was old enough to express himself, they asked him why he was so sad. He replied, "My son was killed in a motorcycle accident." Needless to say, my friends are now firm believers in reincarnation.

If you have a young child, you can try this experiment. When your child is old enough to speak in sentences, ask this question: "Do you remember when you were big?" Then be open to whatever comes.

Chapter 9

Good and Evil

WE ALL HAVE LEARNED to classify things as being good, evil, or neutral. I was no different, until something rather unexpected happened.

I was in a course emphasizing the trance state, under the leadership of Simone Key. The word *trance* has connotations akin to sleepwalking, which is not at all what it is in my world. It starts like any other kind of meditation—you try to achieve a relaxed state of mind and body. After a while, the external world dims until the shuffling in the room and the bird song outside fade away. Some time after that the awareness of your body also fades away. To me it happens in discrete steps, each lasting a few minutes, followed by a steep drop. Ultimately, I am just consciousness floating in an empty void.

For this particular session, our group was meeting with Colin Bates, a tutor for Simone's course. He started us on the road to a trance state, then came to each person and whispered a phrase in their ear. The object of the exercise was to achieve a trance state, and see if a spirit had something to say about the phrase we were given. Later we could present any insights gained in this way to the whole group.

I was in a state of deep relaxation when Colin whispered in my ear, "the creative power of good." It sounded very reasonable and I thought that a spirit would be able to comment on that. It took a while to reach the state of floating in the void. I waited to see if a spirit would give me a message.

Suddenly, a robot appeared about two feet in front of my face, waving its arms frantically shouting "Warning! Danger!" It wasn't just any robot: It was the robot from the television series *Lost in Space*. The series ended in 1968, and I hadn't thought about it in decades. Yet here is this crazy robot telling me there was something wrong with the phrase, "the creative power of good."

There is only one word in that phrase that could possibly cause trouble: the word *good*. Images flooded my mind. I saw Hitler, the crusaders, and airplanes hitting the World Trade Center. Gradually, it made sense. Who gets to define what "good" is? For Hitler, Aryans were good, and everybody else got sent to the camps. For the crusaders, Catholics were good and Muslims could be slaughtered. For the terrorist Muslim extremists who crashed into the twin towers, Muslims were good and infidels could be slaughtered.

Giving Up Duality

In the book of Genesis, there are two chapters that recount the creation story. In the first chapter, man and woman were created at the same time. The world they inhabited gave them everything they wanted without any effort. It was truly paradise. In the second telling, Eve was created from Adam's flesh. Everything was fine until the serpent convinced Eve that in eating from the fruit of the forbidden tree she would know good and evil—and become like God. After she and Adam ate, the story says their eyes were opened and they realized they were naked. Afterwards life became a struggle, the earth didn't cooperate with them, and Eve was cursed with the pain of childbirth.

This old story now had a new meaning for me. If we want to get back to a state of being in which the world cooperates with us, we have to give up the idea of dividing the world into good and evil. We have to give up duality. We have to get back to the verdict that God gave when creation was finished. God saw that it was "very good." Everything is good. Everything has a purpose.

The problem I had with this idea is that there are things that seem evil. Murder isn't good. Child abuse isn't good. There are many more examples. The answer I got was that we need to define everything in terms of *love* rather than *good*. Murder is not a loving thing to do. Child abuse is not a loving thing to do. We can sort out our behavior using this new standard. Hitler's mass murders were not loving. The crusaders were not loving. The terrorists were not loving. *Love* becomes the new yardstick.

The last thing I heard before leaving the trance state was the comment, "Even mosquitoes are good." I'm still trying to accept this even though I think they are worthless pests.

I reported what had happened to my group. When I got home I really tried to embrace the idea that if I gave up duality, the world would cooperate with me. I worked hard to stop making critical judgments, and accept that everything has its purpose. I found that it created a whole new attitude in my life, and I felt much happier and calmer.

The World Cooperates

I had a lease on an Acura that was soon to expire. I had always loved Jaguars, but they were too expensive for me. I decided to ask anyway. I wrote down a list of what I wanted: a Jaguar S-type with a 4.0 liter engine, sport model, sunroof, 6-CD changer, and all the other Jaguar features. It should be platinum gray. It should have at least half its warranty left. Oh, and I can only afford to pay $30,000. I didn't need to ask outright, since making the list was obvious enough. Then I waited, trusting that an answer would come.

I monitored some car sites on the web and found my car on eBay. The auction had several days to run, but being unfamiliar with how these things work, I bid $29,900. A few days later I received an email notifying that I had won the car at my price.

Strangely enough, no one else had bid. It was one year old and had three full years left on its bumper to bumper warranty. The car was in Arizona.

I made arrangements to get the car. Then I realized that I'd have to pay the sales tax back in Indiana to get it registered, and this would exceed my budget. Oops, but this problem took care of itself. The dealer in Arizona gave me an Arizona title for the car. Back in Indiana, I took the title to the Bureau of Motor Vehicles, which informed me that I owed no taxes because I was transferring the car from another state. I still have that car and love it. The sticker price on it was more than $55,000.

A few years later gas prices had more than doubled. The eight cylinders of the Jaguar do like to be fed, and at $4.50 a gallon it was getting really expensive to drive. I had rented a Chevy HHR a few times and really liked the car and its great gas mileage. The car had been produced for less than a year when I decided to put in my request. Used ones were going for more than $16,000. I could afford $10,000. I wrote down the specs. I wanted the LT upper model, not the base LS. It should be dark red with a manual transmission. It should have over half its warranty remaining. Then I released that thought, trusting that Spirit would help. I checked out the car sites on the web once in a while and found my car in Joliet, Illinois. The price was above my limit, but everything else was perfect.

I took a train to Chicago, and my friend Kirt picked me up and drove me to Joliet. I drove the car and really liked it. We did see a small dent in the left rear fender. The dealer then dropped the price. I didn't escape this time without paying the Indiana tax, so the total for the car came to $10,450. Not only did it have over half the normal warranty left, I found out later that it had the factory extended warranty! Thank you Spirit!

I think one of the main lessons is that you have to be specific. Put yourself in the place of the spirit world. You say you need a car. You don't care about the color. You would be happy with any make and model. You just need it to be mechanically sound. If I went out to find a car with that description, I would have no idea where to start. The spirit world would look at this and think, "Well, when you figure out what it is that you want, let us know." You have to be very specific. The more specific you are, the easier it is for the spirit world to locate it for you.

So far this technique has worked for me. The most important thing is to stop calling things evil. What seems like evil to us may have a higher purpose that is beyond our understanding. Act in a loving way. Be specific about what you are asking for. Don't keep nagging them about it. Saying it once is enough. Let it go and trust that it's on its way to you.

I've told the story about my encounter with the robot to several groups. Finally the irony of it dawned on me. Only an engineer would have a robot as a spirit guide!

BOOK FOUR

My Search for Spiritual and Emotional Truths

Chapter 10

My Search for God

THE GREAT UNSOLVED MYSTERY in my life comes from the fact that I have linked with well over 200 people who have passed from life on this planet but who still exist somewhere else. They retain their memories, they still know what's going on in their families, and the bonds of love are as strong as ever. Death does not extinguish consciousness. Even with my skeptical engineering mind, the proof of this has been overwhelming.

So if each of us is in some way immortal, where did we come from? Where is the architect and creator of this whole system? What is its purpose?

The search for God has been going on for centuries. Archeologists all over the world have uncovered figurines representing supernatural entities. Technological societies built elaborate temples with full time employees serving as religious leaders. Some cultures honor their ancestors as playing a role in their current lives. Others honor the forces of nature: the earth from which all food comes, the sky that provides the rain needed for growth, or the storms that frighten them. All of these traditions have stories to explain how the universe works.

Like most people born into our western culture, I was taught that knowledge of God comes from a book, the Bible, which was considered to be the word of God. The Muslim tradition uses the

Quran as their source of revelation. In contrast, religions of the east focus on finding the divine within ourselves through spiritual practices like contemplation and meditation.

Religion is a very personal and sensitive subject. My own path has been full of twists and turns, dead ends, and quantum leaps. My story is unique. I say this because if you are comfortable with your beliefs—and those beliefs include compassion and tolerance—I suggest that you don't abandon them for something unfamiliar.

Until I got into my twenties, I never really thought about any alternatives to the religion my parents practiced. I never questioned or examined the dogmas and beliefs of my religion objectively. I never considered that a totally different spiritual tradition might be a better fit to my beliefs. The friends I made and the social interactions at my church served as a kind of social club, whose members cared about each other and shared common beliefs about spirituality. Trouble started for me when I began researching the history of my church and its beliefs.

My Early Conditioning

I was born into the Roman Catholic tribe. Every Sunday, we piled into the car and went to mass. Catholics have had centuries to develop their rules and beliefs, and somewhere they developed answers for just about any question you could ever ask. It was a mortal sin not to attend mass on Sunday—a sin punished by an eternity in hell. I was a good student, so I studied the catechism, which is the set of dogmas set forth by the church. I learned which sins would land me in hell and which less severe sins would land me in a kind of junior hell called purgatory for a set time based on the severity of my sins. I never questioned any of it.

As part of our education at Saint Joseph Catholic Grade School, we had to attend mass every morning. Upstairs in the choir loft,

Mrs. McCahill—a middle-aged lady with a large family, a generous spirit, and disheveled hair—played the organ and sang the mass. I loved to sing, and I joined the small group of students who sang with her as soon as I could.

When I was in fifth grade, I started piano lessons with Mrs. Rusk—a tall, dark-haired lady whose figure was so thin that she bordered on emaciated. She had two upright pianos in a small room one level down in her house. She chain-smoked while teaching us, but she was a good teacher. Three months after my first lesson she entered me in a competition, and I won. I transferred that skill to the organ at church, learning to use the foot pedals, which resemble a piano keyboard that has been enlarged enough to be played with feet rather than fingers.

I enjoyed this so much that in the summers I'd ride my bike to church in time for the 6:30 A.M. mass and sing with Mrs. McCahill for all four daily masses. Sometimes her son Paul, who was a couple of years older than me, would come too. There was a half-hour break between the second and third masses, so Paul and I would bicycle over to a local deli and have a donut. Encouraged by his large Irish Catholic family, Paul had decided to go to a Catholic seminary for high school, which was located on Notre Dame's campus. The seminary offered a summer camp lasting a week, and as soon as I was old enough, I signed up.

I really enjoyed the atmosphere there. I didn't have any appreciation for what a priest's life would actually be like, but in the Catholic Church the priest had the highest status in the parish. The nuns fawned over them. For a kid looking for some kind of appreciation and who didn't fit in anywhere else, it seemed the right choice. Back in school, while other kids played during the noon recess time, I trained altar boys in the church, pretending to do the mass like the priests did.

When Mrs. McCahill took her summer vacations, I became the organist and singer for all the masses. It was fun for a young kid.

I even composed the march that was used for my eighth-grade graduation ceremony in church.

The Catholic Seminary

After graduation, I could hardly wait until the end of summer and my entry into Holy Cross Seminary. It stood at the top of a hill overlooking St. Mary's Lake, one of two lakes on Notre Dame's campus. The stately, yellow brick building had a T-shaped outline, with the front of the building being the top of the T. That section housed locker rooms downstairs, study halls on the main floor, and two levels of dormitories above. The stem of the T contained hallways leading to an auditorium downstairs, a dining hall on the main floor, and a chapel upstairs. There were less than 100 of us in this high school. Father Nicholas Langenderfer, our Superior (the equivalent of a Principal), was a tall, thin, laid-back priest from California who played the guitar and made us feel at home.

The students lived in three separate areas. Freshmen and sophomores were grouped together in the basement. We had little stalls for our clothes, covered only with a curtain. No one here would ever steal anything. There were two washrooms, each of which had four rows of sinks and mirrors, and a circular shower stall divided into separate sections. The two bathrooms had two rows of separate stalls and a row of urinals. We slept in one of the four dormitories, each containing three rows of beds separated by chairs. The thin mattresses sagged, and the war surplus blankets barely kept us warm. In the morning someone would come in, turn on the lights, and ring a hand bell to wake us.

The juniors had similar facilities in another part of the building. The seniors had their own rooms, two students to a room. While seniors studied in their rooms, the rest of us used the study halls with rows and rows of desks. After breakfast, each of us had housekeeping duties to perform. These were changed every few weeks so no one was stuck with a hard job for a long time. We all ate together in the dining room, called a refectory. Classes were held in a separate building, which also contained a gymnasium, handball court, and some workout equipment upstairs. Shirts and ties were the rule.

I had never learned how to make small talk because I had lived an isolated life, shying away from my peers. Like Pat McKenna said, I knew that I didn't fit in and never tried. Except for recreation periods and class time, we weren't supposed to talk. The quiet appealed to me. I joined the Glee Club, played the organ in the chapel, and learned to play the guitar, forming a singing group with a couple of classmates, playing folk songs at various community gatherings. Except for the mandatory daily sports activities, I felt like I fit in. The only sport that I was any good at was handball. We won't talk about basketball.

The people I lived with were intelligent, and the priests who taught us were talented and supportive. I studied Latin and French in class—and learned Greek on my own. Greek was only taught to juniors and seniors, who would leave notes in Greek on the bulletin board so the underclassmen wouldn't be able to read them. I went to the Dean of Studies and asked to borrow a Greek textbook, and soon I was able to read those notes. In my sophomore year a couple of freshmen also wanted to learn classical Greek, so I started a class and taught them. I've often wondered whether my ease in learning that language was a sign of a previous lifetime in ancient Greece.

At the end of our sophomore year, my class voted to see who would be the president of our junior class. They elected me! I was stunned; it was the first validation I had ever received. The following year I was re-elected president of the senior class.

We were given a lot of opportunities to explore our interests. Because we lived on the campus of Notre Dame, we could also take advantage of events at the university. We were just kids, not little priests, and so there were many fun activities scheduled into the year. One of my favorites was Halloween. The upper class-men would create a house of horrors in the underpinnings of the building, and the rest of us would crawl through it, getting dirty and scared. There was also a projector in the auditorium, and lo-cal theaters would sometimes send a movie over when its run had finished. I looked forward to movie nights, complete with popcorn and soda. We had a good library, a recreation room, an auditorium, and a typing room with three rows of typewriters. In this age of computers, I'm very happy that I took the time to learn how to type. There was also a big secret in the typing room. The screen on one of the windows could swing open like a door.

I remember the time that George Wallace, the governor of Ala-bama, came to the campus to make a speech. He was a racist hid-ing behind the banner of State's Rights, and I wanted to go join the protest. I asked for permission, but my request was denied. I decided to sneak out through the typing-room window. I walked across the campus, was handed a protest sign, and finally went inside to hear his speech. I had to be back in the seminary for night prayer or I'd be missed, so I left the auditorium early. There were a lot of lights outside, but I didn't give them a second thought. I made it back in time.

The next morning I was summoned into the Superior's office. Father William Simmons, the new Superior, looked at me disap-provingly. "I saw you on television last night, John." Oops. Busted! I had no choice but to listen to the verbal lashing.

For some reason I was attracted to foreign languages, espe-cially ones that had strange alphabets. Three of us started to learn Russian together, but we decided later that we wanted to learn He-brew instead. Since the Old Testament is in Hebrew, the faculty thought it was a good idea and promised to find us a teacher. One of the benefactors of the seminary was a Jewish man, Julius Tucker, who would put on a Passover dinner for us every year. He volun-teered to arrange classes for us at Sinai Synagogue in South Bend.

Our teacher was Judah Rosenberg, who was a professor of civil engineering at Notre Dame, and also the cantor at the synagogue. We were allowed to use one of the seminary's cars for the trip into town, where we'd meet once a week at the synagogue. After the class we'd go to Scotty's, the first ten-cent hamburger place in town, and have a hamburger and a shake. Occasionally we would attend the Saturday morning service at Sinai. The alphabet is difficult, the vowels are indicated by little lines and dots, and the sentences go from right to left. I followed along as best I could as they read from the Torah, a hand written scroll containing the first five books of the bible, but they went so fast that I could barely follow the words.

In the process of learning Hebrew, I began to understand the traditions and beliefs that formed the essential background for early Christianity, which grew out of the culture and expectations of the Jewish people.

Looking back on my time in the seminary, I have to admit that I was never a deeply religious person. For me it was about memorizing church history and dogma, which went to my head but not my heart. I never really thought about God much. We were supposed to follow all the rules set out by the church if we wanted to be with God in heaven. I enjoyed the liturgy, the vestments, the ceremonies, and the music that the church had developed over the centuries. It was uplifting, special, and completely different than secular life.

Everything Changes

Then Pope John XXIII convened the Second Vatican Council, which made revolutionary changes in the liturgy. I was a junior when they tore out the communion rail in the chapel, turned the altar around to face the congregation, and abandoned Latin for English at the mass. I was not a happy camper. I loved the ancient Gregorian chant and the grandeur of the old liturgy. In my mind it had been cheapened considerably. The scores of melodies for the various parts of the mass, which I had found so beautiful, were now obsolete. New melodies in English were scarce, so I composed a couple of masses in English to fill the void, and these were adopted by the seminary.

Normally, after graduation from the high school seminary, we would have gone to a farm in Minnesota called a Novitiate. There we would have a year off from conventional studies, with time to think about our futures. At the end of that year, we would take our preliminary vows and become members of the Congregation of Holy Cross. Then we would return to Notre Dame and live at Moreau Seminary for our college years. However, the turmoil after Vatican II had upset those plans. We were sent to St. Joseph Hall on the Notre Dame campus for our first year of college. Boys who wanted to enter the seminary after they graduated from high school elsewhere spent a year there and then proceeded on to the Novitiate. This change of plans happened so quickly that we had to scramble to take the college entrance exams at the last minute.

One of the advantages of the chaos was that our status at Notre Dame permitted me to sign up for courses that I wanted to take, as opposed to having my schedule dictated. I signed up for a philosophy course that was restricted to juniors on the Dean's List. Even though history was my worst subject, I also signed up for honors history, because the teacher, Matthew Fitzsimons, was a legend. I skipped the science course I was supposed to take and signed up for Greek, Latin, and Hebrew courses. My Hebrew class conflicted with a mandatory weekly meeting back at St. Joseph Hall. The old priest who mumbled through those talks was notoriously boring, so I was happy to have an excuse not to attend. One day he changed the way a certain chapel service would be conducted. As it turned out, I was leading the service that evening. I did it the old way because I didn't know any better. That night there appeared a note in poorly written Hebrew on the bulletin board. It translated,

"Ears bread and do not hear." I took my pen and corrected it to read, "They have ears and do not hear," a quote from the Bible. From his reaction you'd think I had just pooped on a photograph of the Pope. I was castigated for taking Hebrew instead of being at the weekly lectures. The clear anti-Semitic tone made me angry.

The Seed of Doubt

Having the proper language skills, I was looking forward to translating the original text of the New Testament, which was written in Greek. However, I found it strange that the text was in Greek rather than Aramaic, the common language among the Jewish people in Palestine at that time.

As I looked into it more, I was surprised to learn that there is no original text. Like most other Christians, I had assumed that the four gospels were written by eyewitnesses who had followed Jesus around and recorded his words. This was far from the truth. No one knew who wrote the gospels. The names Matthew, Mark, Luke, and John were given to the gospels much later to give them more authority. The oldest complete copies we have today date from the fourth century. Before then there were many individual gospels—and many different opinions on who Jesus was and what he taught. The earliest gospels were written decades after Jesus died. Until then there were probably stories about him passed on verbally. Anyone who has played the children's game called telephone knows how garbled things become as they are passed along.

Upon close examination, it became clear to me that the gospels are not eyewitness accounts. Nowhere does it say things like "we went" or "we saw." Whoever wrote the gospel attributed to Luke was probably not even Jewish. Mark even got the geography of Israel wrong.

Each of the gospel texts were reproduced by individuals who copied them by hand and passed them on. Not only were many copying mistakes made, but the texts were modified extensively to reflect the biases of the copyists. The people who produced these writings were not historians but salesmen. The texts were designed to convince people that the Jewish messiah had come. Words were added, subtracted, and changed. In fact, whole paragraphs were added. Matthew and Luke copied Mark, which is the oldest gospel, and added additional material. The gospel of John was written much later and has a totally different point of view.

I learned that there were more than a dozen other gospels that I had never heard of. There were gospels according to the Hebrews, the Egyptians, the Twelve Apostles—not to mention the gospels of Judas Iscariot, of Peter, of Valentinus, of Marcion, of Basilides, of Thomas, of Matthias, of Tatian, of Bartholomew, of Philip, of the Nazarenes, of Jude, of Nicodemus, of Andrew—and who knows how many others that have been lost. Then there are many books titled the Acts of so-and-so and a dizzying group of letters (epistles). The four gospels we find today probably did not take their present form until the end of the second century. There were heated debates about which ones should be declared "official." The first document that proposes a New Testament composed of today's twenty-seven elements dates to 367.

In 380 the Emperor Theodosius issued an edict stating that anyone who disagreed with the Roman definition of Christianity "will be branded with the ignominious name of heretic" and "will suffer ... the punishment of our authority." Consequently, dissenting bishops were deposed, their churches were closed, and competing gospels were destroyed.

The winners were the four gospels we all know. The oldest copies we have date to the fourth century. One is a copy kept in the Vatican since the fifteenth century. It's called *Vaticanus*. The other was found at the Monastery of St. Catherine in the Sinai, although pieces of it ended up in four institutions. This document is called *Sinaiticus*. Two authoritative copies from the same century ought to be alike. Yet there are 656 differences in Matthew, 567 in Mark, 791 in Luke, and 1022 in John.

Contrast this to Jewish texts. When a scribe copies a scroll, it is done with great care. If two letters touch each other, the scroll becomes invalid. For that reason, when old copies of Jewish scriptures are unearthed, like those in the Dead Sea scrolls, they are nearly identical to what we have today. In the Isaiah scroll only ten letters are different, and these were due to spelling differences. Hebrew has two letters for "S" and two for "T'"

I began this study because I was motivated to understand the original meaning of the gospels, but gradually I understood that the texts we were reading in church were selected from dozens of options and edited heavily over time. I found this deeply disturbing, even threatening.

I studied the Dead Sea Scrolls, written around a time when the authors were expecting a final showdown between the forces of light (observant Jews) and the forces of evil (Romans and their Jewish puppets). Revolutionary fever was in the air. It was a chaotic time in the Middle East. The Jews living in Palestine greatly resented the Romans, who demanded heavy taxes and who worshipped forbidden gods. They even appointed the high priest of the temple, which meant that large groups of the population felt that the temple had been profaned and corrupted. Surely God would not let this continue much longer.

There were many individuals preaching about this coming battle and the emergence of a new Jewish king, ruling from a newly sanctified Jerusalem. The Hebrew word for "messiah," translated as *christos* in Greek, actually means someone anointed with oil. The name Jesus Christ should be translated as "Jesus the Anointed." The kings of Israel were messiahs, anointed to lead the nation. The new king would be descended from David, who came from Bethlehem. Any candidate for a new messiah would have to be his descendant.

Who Was Jesus?

The story of Jesus' birth in Bethlehem is found in Matthew and Luke. Matthew simply states that Jesus was born in Bethlehem, as though Joseph had always lived there. Luke says that Joseph came from Nazareth. Both give genealogies for Joseph, but they are completely different and do not even agree on who Joseph's father was. After Jesus was born, Matthew takes the family from Bethlehem to Egypt until King Herod dies. A dream makes him afraid to go home to Bethlehem, so he moves to Nazareth. Luke has the family leave Nazareth, travel to Bethlehem to participate in a census, and move on to Jerusalem after Jesus was born to fulfill Jewish laws concerning the birth of the first son and purification of the mother. After that, they returned to Nazareth. The accounts cannot be reconciled.

The doctrine of the virginity of Mary comes from a mistranslation of a Hebrew word that actually means "young lady." The literal translation reads, "The young lady is pregnant," but it refers to the mother of a Jewish prophet centuries earlier. After this doctrine was promulgated, references to Joseph as Jesus' father were edited out, which makes Joseph's elaborate genealogies in Matthew and Luke rather nonsensical.

Matthew and Luke both describe how angels, shepherds, and even wise men with expensive gifts visited Jesus after his birth. But Mark tells the story of how his family tried to take Jesus away because they thought he was crazy. In another passage, when Jesus went back to Nazareth, the people there did not respect him. If all these amazing things that Matthew and Luke spoke of at the time of his birth had actually occurred, Jesus would have been esteemed and honored, not rejected.

As each of these things became clear to me, I found myself feeling disillusioned. It felt as though I had been tricked, and thirteen years of Catholic education began to seem more like brainwashing.

I began to wonder whether Jesus had really intended to start a new religion. There are 613 commandments in the Torah, the first five books of the bible. The Catholic church and most other varieties of Christianity basically threw most of these commandments in the trash. The Old Testament was replaced with the New. Old rules no longer applied. Why?

Both Matthew and Luke address the issue of whether Jesus abandoned or changed Jewish law. Certain letters in the Torah scroll wear little crowns. They are tiny decorations added to the tops of some letters. Matthew states, "Do not suppose that I came to demolish the law or the prophets. I come not to demolish, but to fulfill them … . I solemnly tell you, until the sky and the earth disappear, not one iota or one tiny stroke of the law will go away until everything will come to be." The Greek text refers to the letter iota because it is the smallest letter of the Greek alphabet. The corresponding letter in Hebrew is yod, which is not much bigger than a comma. The tiny strokes refer to the little decorations. So what this statement means is that not the smallest letter or even the decorations on the letters will pass away. The passage continues, "Therefore whoever breaks the smallest of these commandments and teaches men likewise will be called least in the kingdom of heaven, but who keeps them and teaches them will be called great in the kingdom of heaven."

Luke makes it more succinct: "It would be easier for heaven and earth to disappear than for one little stroke to drop out of the law." To me this didn't sound like a person who wants to reject Judaism and start another religion.

Another passage convinced me that Jesus was not interested in converting others. Matthew states, "Jesus sent these twelve out with these instructions: Do not go to gentile nations, and do not enter any Samaritan town. Go instead to the lost sheep of the house of Israel … announce that the kingdom of heaven is close at hand."

So what was the message that Jesus was teaching? Mark, the oldest gospel, doesn't begin with an elaborate genealogy or singing angels but with the statement that Jesus came from Nazareth and was baptized in the Jordan by John the Baptist. After John was arrested, Mark states that Jesus went back to Galilee, and started preaching. "The time is fulfilled, and the kingdom of God has come near. Repent, and have faith in the good news."

Isaiah and many later prophets had promised a time when God would abolish all the pagan influences and set up a Jewish kingdom that would be respected worldwide. John the Baptist, and Jesus his follower, wanted people to know that this was going to happen soon. John was using immersion in the Jordan river as a sign of purity and rededication to the Torah in preparation for the coming kingdom of God.

There were many other people predicting the end of the world at this turbulent time. Collectively they are called apocalyptic prophets, and Jesus was one of them. They preached the violent end of the world as they knew it, and the establishment of a new world order based on God's Torah.

Evidence for this can be found in Mark, where Jesus paraphrases the prophet Joel. "In those days following the distress, the sun will be darkened, and the moon will not give its light, the stars will fall from the sky, and the heavenly bodies will be shaken." When will all this happen? And Jesus answers, "Truly I tell you, before this generation has passed away all these things will have taken place."

Some Jews expected that when the new messiah came, the righteous dead would rise from the grave in order to participate in this joyous time that their obedience to God's laws helped bring about. I found this curious passage in Matthew: "And the tombs were opened, and many bodies of the holy people who had fallen asleep were raised. And coming forth out of the tombs after their rising, they went into the holy city and appeared to many."

The belief that Jesus rose from the dead is at the core of Christianity. But when I put the resurrection stories in the four gospels side by side, I find no agreement on who went to the tomb, what they saw, or what happened afterwards. In one version Jesus appears to his followers in Jerusalem; in another they had to go to Galilee first. They have different people going to the tomb, seeing different things, and doing different things afterwards. The gospel attributed to John says that Mary Magdalene saw Jesus but thought he was the gardener. If my sister rose from the dead, I know I'd recognize her.

From my present perspective, I can't dismiss the possibility that Jesus was seen after he died. After all, I can see dead people too. In the next chapter, I will tell you the story of a Hawaiian woman who was as solid as I am but who disappeared into thin air. The contradictory accounts of the resurrection suggest to me that the four authors invented these accounts in order to explain how some people saw Jesus after his death.

After the Romans killed Jesus, his brother James took over as the leader of the movement. These followers of Jesus were called Nazarenes or Ebionites, from a word meaning "poor people." These were the people who knew Jesus best, who heard him speak, who knew his teachings. They had their own gospels, copies of which have not yet been discovered, although we know they existed because they are mentioned in other documents.

The Ebionites believed that Jesus was a flesh and blood human, conceived and born in the normal way, and that Joseph was his father. They also believed that he was the Jewish messiah who was sent to the Jews to set up a Jewish nation. His devotion to God's laws as set forth in the Torah earned him a special status. But the idea that Jesus himself was God would be totally foreign to any Jew. The most important statement in Judaism is this: "Hear O Israel, YHVH is our God, YHVH alone." The whole faith rests on the belief in a single, invisible God. This distinguished the Jews from all the other cultures around them, who worshiped multiple gods. Catholics believe that there is one God who has three manifestations. I could never understand that. Jesus prayed in the garden of Gethsemane. Who was he praying to? Would one part of God have to suffer and die to convince another part of the same God to forgive mankind?

The Romans Create a New Religion

Pondering these things completely changed the way I thought about the New Testament and the doctrines that the Catholic church had taught me. Even the idea of Sunday as the assigned day for worship began to bother me. The Hebrew word *Shabbat* is a day of the week, namely, Saturday. To say that the Sabbath is on Sunday makes as much sense as saying Wednesday is on Thursday.

James, the brother of Jesus, led the movement in Jerusalem after Jesus was put to death. But the Jewish revolt of 66 C.E. and the subsequent destruction of the Jewish temple by Titus in 70 C.E. ended the influence of Jerusalem as the center of Jewish worship. Surely the end of the whole world was not far off.

His followers remembered Jesus' words and expected the end of the world in their own lifetimes. As that generation died off, the message was reinterpreted. The central figure in this transformation was a Jew named Saul, who took the Roman name Paul. Paul had never met Jesus and had never heard him preach. Yet the bulk of the New Testament consists of writings attributed to Paul. Paul is not shy about his status. His first letter to the Galatians starts with this: "I want you to know, brothers and sisters, that the gospel I preached is not of human origin. I did not receive it from any man, nor was I taught it; rather, I received it by revelation from Jesus Christ."

Wow. That's a pretty bold statement. Paul is saying that it did not matter to him what Jesus said and did, because he had his own direct line of communication with the messiah. Having freed himself from the historical life and teachings of Jesus, he goes on to create his own theology.

Paul's message angered both observant Jews and Jesus' followers in Jerusalem, led by James. But it appealed to Hellenized Jews and pagans. Circumcision was the mark of the covenant with God and his people and had been observed for centuries. But the Greeks considered it mutilation. For Paul to make converts among them, he preached against the practice. This further alienated Jews, so Paul turned to the gentiles, who saw the world of gods in a totally different way. Over the next 200 years, Jesus became not a son of God, a Jewish term meaning someone God selected to perform a specific task, but the true offspring of a god with a human woman. There were many legends among the gentiles of these demi-gods, like Hercules. Jesus was reinterpreted as God made flesh. This was the final split with Judaism, whose entire religion was based on the principle that there is only one God, not two or three.

In the end, the religion of Christianity was defined in pagan Rome by people who had forgotten or rejected its Jewish origins. The emperor Constantine demanded a clearly defined set of documents forming the foundation for this new religion. Going through all the gospels and letters that had multiplied immensely since the time of Jesus, church leaders selected the edited versions of four stories, along with some letters of Paul, some real, some forged, a few other letters, and the book of Revelation. The rest of the documents were banned. We have some of these banned books because they were buried rather than burned. A central authority was set up in Rome to define and control the theology as it saw fit—and to approve and appoint the leaders of the Christian movement, backed by the force and authority of the Roman government. In a final irony, the Ebionites, who were closest to the teachings of Jesus, were condemned as heretics, which is why we no longer have their gospel.

The more I learned the less respect I had for the Catholic church. The subsequent history of the church included massacring thousands of innocent Muslims during the crusades—and the destruction of all the cultures of Central and South America in the name of Christianity. When I left St. Joseph Hall at the end of my freshman year, I left the Catholic church behind as well.

There are many things in the New Testament to admire and respect. Loving your enemies, helping the sick and the poor, making no judgments against others—these are the values we should all aspire to. They are rooted in Judaism. While I could no longer accept the legitimacy of the Catholic church, I still embraced the compassionate themes of the New Testament.

Embracing Judaism

For a while I enjoyed not going to church on Sundays. But the desire was still there to do some form of spiritual practice. I decided to convert to Judaism. I went back to Sinai Synagogue where I had studied Hebrew, and spoke with Rabbi Alan Kuperman. He was a young rabbi who had a full beard, rode a motorcycle, and had a great sense of humor. When I would ask him a difficult question about one of the Torah's commandments, he'd reply that he was in sales, not management.

Over the next year Alan and I became close friends in spite of the fact that I questioned everything I was being taught. I was always invited for dinner at his home on Friday nights, joining his wife Judy and their two children. Judy would light two candles and recite the blessing that began *Shabbat,* and a festive meal followed. Since he was an Orthodox rabbi, my conversion would also be Orthodox.

One of the great differences between Jews and Roman Catholics is the status of the rabbi. A Catholic priest had special powers—forgiving sins in confession, changing water and wine into flesh and blood, performing the sacraments. A rabbi has no such

powers. He is a highly trained specialist in Jewish law and traditions, more like a lawyer than a priest, and is there to explain or
answer any questions about proper Jewish practices. Any member
of the congregation can lead the services because all are equal.

Another difference stood out for me. The Catholic faith focused
on an afterlife, with the idea that this life was a test to see if you
were good enough to go to heaven. Jews have no doctrine concerning an afterlife. Some Jews think that this life is all there is, some
believe in reincarnation, and some think of something similar to
the Christian heaven. Since there is no doctrine, you can believe
whatever you want. The emphasis in Judaism is on this life.

Judaism doesn't care what your beliefs are. What matters is
what you do, not what you think. This was one of the big fights
between Saul/Paul and James, who led Jesus' followers in Jerusalem. Judaism takes the words of God as recorded in the Torah very
seriously. Take for example this passage: "Fix these words of mine
in your hearts and minds; tie them as symbols on your hands and
bind them on your foreheads. Teach them to your children, talking
about them when you sit at home and when you walk along the
road, when you lie down and when you get up. Write them on the
doorframes of your houses and on your gates." Jews take these
commands seriously, following an oral tradition that explains how
to obey them. If you enter a Jewish home you can see a small de-
vice called a *mezuzah* affixed to the door frame. You may also have
seen pictures of Jews wearing little boxes, one tied to the left arm
close to the heart and one fixed on the forehead, as instructed by
this passage from Deuteronomy. Inside all these devices are small
scrolls containing quotes from the Torah. If God said to do something, you did it as best you could. Paul thought that while these
things applied to Jews, foreigners didn't need to comply; if you
believed in Jesus as the messiah, you didn't need to do anything
else.

About a year later Alan decided I was ready for the formal

conversion. Since I had been circumcised at birth, tradition required a single drop of blood instead. Rabbi Bergman came to
Alan's office and with a needle drew a single drop of blood from
my foreskin. This had to be witnessed by two adults, and a letter
was written in Hebrew confirming the procedure. I was relieved
that it didn't hurt. The next day we drove to Chicago, where rabbis
from the Chicago Rabbinical Council conducted an interview to
make sure I was ready. They reminded me that Jews have been re-
viled and persecuted over their history, and asked me if I was willing to throw my lot in with them regardless of what might happen
in the future. I was. Then they took me to the *mikvah*, which is a
pool of water used for purification, and standing there naked, I re-
cited a blessing then submerged myself in the pool. The Christian
practice of baptism is derived from this tradition. Afterwards they
filled out a form in Hebrew, and I was officially Jewish.

Although I was not living at home at the time, I decided to tell
my mother that I had converted to Judaism. She quickly objected,
"Jews don't believe in God." I reminded her of Moses and the Ten
Commandments. "Well, they don't believe in something." Mom
thought she was always right, never mind the facts.

I became an active member of Sinai Synagogue. I studied with
Cantor Israelov, learning the musical phrases that are used to recite the *haftarah,* which is a reading from the prophets. I learned to
lead the Friday night services welcoming *Shabbat.* My friendship
with the Kuperman family continued to grow. I even took care of
their two children when Judy went into the hospital to deliver their
third baby. They were my best friends.

One day at the Friday night dinner, Alan told me that they had
decided to move to Israel. I was crushed. While I could understand
their desire to play a part in rebuilding a Jewish state, I knew that
it would leave a huge hole in my heart and in my life. The dreaded
day finally came when they packed up and left.

I exchanged cassette tape recordings with my friend Alan in

Israel, keeping in touch. Judy was pregnant with their fourth child. They were building their own house in a settlement east of Jerusalem, which ran into many problems. Then one morning while taking a shower, Alan dropped dead. He was thirty-eight years old. I helped organize a memorial service for him at Sinai and could not get over the feeling of guilt that I had never gone to Israel to visit the family after they moved.

A Moral Dilemma

At this time in my life I built my first computer and began analyzing airfoils as a hobby. Well known airplane designer Burt Rutan had used one of my designs on a self-launching glider called Solitaire, and now asked me to design wings for an airplane that would try to circumnavigate the earth on a single tank of gas. Suddenly I was very busy. I had been making a living working with a close friend as an independent steel broker, but I soon began spending all my free time working on these aerodynamic designs. A couple of years later I was under contract to Beech Aircraft working on the design of a business turboprop called Starship, had two employees, and was spending months traveling. My attendance at Sinai became very infrequent.

After four years under contract to Beech, I was working as an independent consultant and had plenty of work. I had won a competition to design a new small jet airplane, but as we crunched the numbers it became apparent that the plane was not viable with the engines they intended to use. I held a meeting at their headquarters, and spent several hours going through all the work we had done, explaining why the airplane was underpowered. There was simply no way to make it work.

They decided to proceed anyway. It was a moral dilemma for me. I was being treated really well. For example, the company would send a private jet to pick me up at the local airport and bring me back. I was being well paid. But I knew that the project was doomed. Do I continue taking their money while knowing that the project would fail? I decided that I could not in conscience do that, so I resigned from the project. Shortly after that I found a five-week cruise from Athens to Cape Town and called my friend Tim who thought about it for a minute then said "Okay, I'll go" and soon we were flying to Greece.

Learning about Buddhism

Since there were many days at sea, I brought a few books. One was called *The Art of Happiness* by the Dalai Lama. I had read about him, and was intrigued with the fact that he was selected as the reincarnation of the thirteenth Dalai Lama. They had proved this while he was a young toddler when he was able to select many objects that the previous Dalai Lama had owned. I thought this was amazing. There had to be something to the idea of reincarnation.

The teachings of the Buddha (awakened one) impressed me as well. One of the quotes that sticks with me even now says, "All unhappiness comes from refusing to accept what is." That phrase has served me well. When I'm feeling unhappy, the first thing I ask myself is what fact I'm refusing to accept.

Another great lesson of Buddhism is detachment. We get attached to all sorts of things, and then our happiness becomes dependent on them. I found it challenging at first to enjoy things without becoming attached to them. If a tree drops on my car, destroying it, I would miss the car, but I would still be okay. In our materialistic culture life often seems like a race to accumulate things. I have learned that in the end those things ended up owning me. The more stuff I can live without, the happier I become. I gave my boat away for free to a family that couldn't afford one. I sold my airplane at a ridiculously low price to someone who loved it and can maintain it.

The Buddhist quality I strive for is compassion. If I see a disabled person, I ask Spirit to bless him. If I see a rusted out car my instant reaction is that these people have no money for a better one, and it rouses my compassion for them. Buddhists also have respect for all forms of life. So yes, I try to move spiders and such outdoors rather than smashing them. Buddhism is not a religion, because God is never mentioned in Buddhist teaching. It is a philosophy on how to live.

Buddhists also believe in reincarnation, as do the Jewish mystics called Kabbalists. I've studied their works extensively. Being a skeptical engineer, I've also looked at the scientific evidence: children who start speaking a language unknown to their parents; children who display advanced talents at a very young age; children who can actually remember their previous lives, locate the house where they used to live and even where their toys were kept. Good research material is readily available, much of which is very technical and boring. In the end I came to accept reincarnation as scientific fact. Since I began working with mediumship, I have encountered a few examples of being shown someone's previous lifetime, especially how they passed away, which can lead to some problems in their current lifetimes. I find it much easier to accept the tragedies in life knowing that we all come back.

My Introduction to Spiritualism

Finally, when I attended the Arthur Findlay College I was introduced to Spiritualism. It is a recognized religion in England, with equal status to other denominations like Presbyterians or Methodists. There are many Spiritualist churches in England. The College has two Spiritualist services in the Sanctuary each week. One of the main parts of the service features mediums who give messages to members of the congregation from their dead family and friends. The College is designed to train these mediums.

These are the seven principles of Spiritualism:

- We all come from the same Great Central Force
- We are all brothers and sisters in one big family
- The communion of spirits and spirit helpers
- The continuous existence of the human soul
- Personal responsibility
- Compensation and retribution for the deeds done on earth
- Eternal progress is open to every soul

The communion of spirits affirms that communication is possible between the living and those who have died. Love never dies. We are also provided with helpers from the spirit world. Some call them guides or angels. They help us in this lifetime, and although Spiritualism doesn't explicitly embrace the concept of reincarnation, I believe that our team on the other side helps us to plan our future lives and helps us meet the goals we set for ourselves when we come into this lifetime. Each lifetime has a lesson plan, and this world and other worlds serve as classrooms.

I read a description of this process that I like very much. Raw diamonds look like rough rocks. Only after a skilled polisher begins to cut the diamond, and polish each facet, does it become a highly prized gem. Our souls are like that. Each facet is a lifetime, and if we meet the challenge we set out to face, one facet gets polished. Through this process we will become a perfect gem.

The Spiritualist principle of personal responsibility rules out blaming somebody else for the things we do. We make our own choices. But we all know good people who have suffered tragically through no fault of their own. Those people will receive compensation when they reach the spirit world. On the other hand if a person has done a lot of hateful actions, they will receive retribution.

The final principle means that even Adolph Hitler will have a chance to become a better person. This is very unlike the Catholic concept of going to hell for all eternity. Instead, through facing hardships in new lifetimes, his soul is open to progress too.

So at this point in my life, I describe myself as a Jewish/Buddhist/Spiritualist, and really find no contradictions in that. Instead, I find them complementary.

"God"

So after this long journey, when I say the word *God*, what does it mean to me?

In the end, I combined the mystic vision of Kabbalah with a scientific twist. For me God is *Ein-Sof*, Hebrew for "without end". It describes a power that is hidden and unknowable, completely beyond human comprehension. *Ein-Sof* constantly creates our physical world, as a way of turning abstract ideas into physical reality. In this way *Ein-Sof* comes to know itself.

At first it seems hard to understand that. But without a physical world, whatever potential abilities or talents that exist cannot be realized. These abilities would remain just unrealized potential. God is the source of all potential, and I think the physical world is continuously created in order to express and explore that potential. *Ein-Sof* is experiencing itself through us and through all of creation.

There is a scientific explanation for how that works. I was taught that space is a vacuum. But it turns out that what we call a vacuum is in fact a boiling soup of electrodynamic waves, producing quantum particles that come into and out of existence continuously. They are called "virtual particles." You can prove that they exist by placing two flat plates very close to each other. The virtual particles will push the plates towards each other. In fact, most of the weight you see when you step on a scale comes from these virtual particles. Protons and neutrons are made up of three smaller particles called quarks. The little quarks are bound together by a force made up of gluons (I love that name). But gluons have no mass at all, and the mass of the quarks is only about 1/80 of the mass of a proton or neutron. The other 98+ percent comes from the energy supplied by the virtual particles boiling out of the gluons to bind the quarks together. By Einstein's equation, energy is equivalent to mass, so all that energy weighs far more than the little quarks.

To me, the quantum vacuum is the fingerprint of God. Its dense soup of virtual particles is the stuff out of which anything can be made, and which makes existence possible. If you could turn off the quantum vacuum, the universe would fall apart. I think of this invisible force as a Divine Power Grid. To me that power is totally nonjudgmental. An analogy might be the electricity in your wall outlets. It will power all kinds of devices, but it makes no judgments about how you use that power.

So why do I bother to drive an hour every day to attend the afternoon services at my synagogue? Why do I refuse to eat pork and keep the other Jewish traditions? If God is not keeping score, why bother? I choose to do these things because I want to remind myself that I am a soul having a human experience. I am spirit, and in doing these things I honor that spirit. It's about me—remembering who I am, rather than fearing some kind of divine punishment or expecting divine applause.

God's powerhouse permits us to create both loving and hateful things. It's our challenge to choose love over hate, and we have many lifetimes to achieve this. As I explained previously, if we hurt people then we will feel that pain when we cross over. If we make people happy, we will feel that joy as well.

I know that we have a team of spirits working with us. Some have watched us through many lifetimes, and some are there just when we are working at something. I'm convinced that my unusual success with aerodynamics is partly due to unseen helpers in the other world putting ideas in my head. I rely on these *inspirations*. The word itself means "in spirit." When I pray for something, I think it's my spirit team that replies, using the Divine Power Grid to effect an answer.

If I'm right, then everything we see, everything we measure, all the parallel and unseen universes, all dark matter and all dark energy, are manifestations of God. We are all part of that manifestation. In that way, we are all The One.

Chapter 11

My Search for Love

IN THE EARLY PART of the book of Genesis, God is quoted as saying "It is not good for man to be alone." The search for someone to love, and someone to love us back, occupies much of our lives. Think of all the television programs and movies whose plots revolve around that search.

I grew up feeling inadequate—and feeling that I didn't belong. I dodged all the dating issues for five years by going to a Catholic seminary.

Since priests don't get married, there was never any talk about who was dating whom, or which girl had the biggest boobs, or similar conversations you'd find in a regular high school. So I never dealt with the issue at all.

A Night in Chicago

A senior named Mike was the smartest person in the school. I was a freshman at the time, and I really admired him. He was a bit shy like me—and brilliant. But there was little opportunity to interact. The recreation room was divided. Juniors and seniors were on one side, freshmen and sophomores on the other. Seniors did not hang out with freshmen, so the only contact I had with Mike was in the music room. We both enjoyed classical music, and I always found a question I could ask Mike about Greek grammar or some composer.

By the time I was a senior, Mike was in college, living at Moreau Seminary, where college level seminarians lived. He called me one day and asked me if I wanted to go to Chicago with him. I jumped at the chance because we had never had a long conversation in high school. He didn't have access to a car, so I called my mother and asked her if I could borrow hers. She let me have the car, and Mike drove us to Chicago, his home town. We went to a bar in Old Town. Since I was not twenty-one, Mike brought a classmate's driver's license. I didn't think I looked much like him, and it made me nervous when a guard at the door looked at it with a flashlight, then shined the light on me. He let us in. Whew!

We talked a lot about college classes, number theory, and many other things. It felt wonderful to be with my former hero. We had a couple of drinks. I had never had much alcohol before, and I was feeling it. Sometime after midnight we went back to the car and headed for home, an hour-and-half away. Mike stopped at a liquor store and went in. He emerged with a bottle of champagne and two Styrofoam cups. He parked the car on the side of the road leading home and popped the cork, pouring champagne for both of us. I had always wondered what champagne tasted like, and I liked it. But the late hour and the alcohol finally got to me, and I fell asleep. I was awakened later by the sound of a police siren. Mike had been weaving a bit. The policeman saw the champagne bottle in the car and asked for our IDs. I dug for my proper ID. My hands were shaking. We were very close to a service plaza, and the policeman let us go, instructing us to go inside and have some coffee. When we got there, I had a hard time holding the cup because I was still shaking.

We made it back to the parish where Mike was staying. He got out of the car, walked away, walked back as if he wanted to say something, hesitated then walked away again. Some months after that Mike committed suicide. I did not realize for a long time what had really gone on that night. Mike had taken me on my first date. I was just too naive to figure it out. Even if I had understood, it would not have worked at that time because I hadn't faced my own sexuality. Sometimes, I still go to the cemetery and lay a flower on his grave. John Holland had linked with him during my first mediumistic reading.

Out on My Own

Back in the early sixties, the only thing I knew about gay people was that they wanted to wear women's clothes and molest little boys. Clearly I had no interest in either of those things, so I could not possibly be gay. I thought that some of my classmates were very handsome, but I never thought of them in that way.

As I explained in an earlier chapter, for my first year of college I moved to St. Joseph Hall on the Notre Dame campus. My classmates from the high school seminary joined new students who came into the program starting at the college level. The culture clash between those of us who had spent four years together and those just starting was disturbing. The priest in charge was very conservative, so much so that sometimes I wondered whether he had been flash frozen in the dark ages and thawed out just to aggravate us. We chafed under his rule. During the year, several of my high school classmates left. At the end of the year almost everyone left. I was among them.

I was old enough to realize that I wasn't interested in performing the duties of a priest; I just wanted the status. I wanted to be respected, to be validated. I also liked being with my classmates, who had elected me to be their leader. With most of them gone, I no longer had a motive to continue.

When I moved back home, Dad issued a command: "You have to start dating." I resented being told what to do, and at this point in my life I had a lot of other questions to ponder, like what to do for a living. I had never thought about that either. I had felt secure and safe in the seminary environment. Now I had to deal with the outside world, and the prospect made me nervous.

The previous summer I had been an intern at the *South Bend Tribune,* and I really enjoyed the experience and thought that I might pursue journalism. I found that the Rochester Institute of Technology in New York had a highly respected program. Jack Fahey flew me out to see the school in his Comanche. I liked what I saw, and I enrolled.

It was my first time out in the real world. I felt really awkward, almost like being in a foreign country. I was used to being with people who had been together for four or five years and knew each other well, and I found it hard to make small talk with strangers. I did make friends with Mike, a classmate, and his wife Fran. I'd stop there in the morning on the way to school, and Fran would make us hot biscuits and coffee. I didn't fit in very well with my other classmates. Their experiences and interests were totally different than mine. I did good work in school and got good grades, but I just didn't fit in. I kept to myself.

I did quite a bit of creative photography and writing at school. I lived in a cheap apartment in a ghetto, and I got to know and photograph the neighborhood kids. Some of the photos were selected for publication in a magazine. It was the age of hippies. I did try marijuana sometimes with classmates, but it never affected me at all except to give me a headache. Everyone else got high; I got sick. I tried to fit in, but it never worked.

The courses at the college were not very challenging, and I was bored. I decided to return to Notre Dame for the last two years of college. Most of my credits transferred. Dad decided that I should become a lawyer. He had lawyer friends that he could persuade to hire me. I really didn't have any good ideas of my own, so I majored in Government and International Studies. Dad figured it was cheaper to add a room above the television room than to pay room and board on campus, which meant finally I had my own room at home. I'd drive to school in the used VW Beetle I had bought with the pay from my summer job at the newspaper. While I was good at learning, I had not yet found anything that ignited any passion in me. Still, I managed to graduate with honors,

Then it was time for law school, also at Notre Dame. It was incredibly boring. We had to read case after case, trying to understand the principles that the court used to make decisions. I hated it—and I was miserable. In the basement at home Dad had a liquor cabinet. I started raiding it. One day my parents caught me in the basement drinking and yelled at me. I finally said to them, "Do you want to know what's wrong?"

They looked at me and said, "No", and quickly walked upstairs, Dad was more worried about the cost of the liquor, I thought. They did not care about me at all.

In my contract law class, we had a case involving a lady who had bought some items from a department store on time payments. The contract said that until she paid off the total amount, they still legally owned those items. She had nearly paid off the bill when she lost her job and missed some payments. The store took back everything she had ever bought from them, citing the contract. The court ruled in favor of the store. I complained in class about the totally unfair ruling. The professor argued law. I argued fairness.

Finally, he was fed up with my objections. "Mr. Roncz," he said, "what you'll never get through your fat skull is that the law has nothing to do with justice."

Wow. I went to see the Dean of the Law School. He looked at my transcript and asked me why, with all these varied interests, I had come to law school. Basically, because my father made me. He said that if I hated law school, I would hate being a lawyer even more. I agreed. I withdrew from law school.

I could not bring myself to tell Dad. I drove to the library every morning and stayed there until my usual time to return home. The jig was up, however, when Dad got a letter about a partial refund of the tuition. He reacted by throwing all my things out the window onto the driveway. I picked them up and went to live with Grandma Roncz. I told her what had happened. She got on the phone and cussed out my father in Hungarian. Eventually, I was allowed to return home.

Dad owned a metal stamping business. His secretary had been injured in an auto accident, and he ordered me to go to work for him and clean up the huge backlog of paperwork. I reorganized the office, invented a better way to keep track of orders, and liked the other people I worked with. I stayed on there, and was promoted to purchasing agent. I saved up enough money to put a down payment on a house in 1987. Finally, I had my own home.

A New Career Taking Off

The new Heathkit catalog came offering a microprocessor-based computer kit. I had to have one. I soldered all the wires and eventually had a working computer. Back in high school, I had bought a book called *The Theory of Wing Sections,* which described the design and testing of many shapes of airplane wings. I loved airplanes, but the math was beyond me. Now that I had a computer, I decided to write a program to solve some of the equations in that book. By changing the variables and studying the results, I taught myself airfoil theory.

Every summer in Oshkosh, Wisconsin, there is a huge aviation convention held by the Experimental Aircraft Association. They sold plans for building your own airplanes. I had admired the designs of a California engineer named Burt Rutan, and I bought plans for one of his airplanes called VariEze. I took careful measurements of the wing airfoil section from the plans and analyzed the shape using my new computer. I sent him the results. At that time, he was looking at several shapes for a new glider he was designing. I volunteered to do the same kind of analysis on those shapes. I hand-drew plots of the results and made a tape recorded commentary so that he could follow along. By this time I had already designed airfoil sections of my own, and I threw these in also. Burt chose to use my design rather than the ones he had sent me. The airplane flew well. This started a relationship that lasted many years and produced many unique designs.

The first few airplanes I worked on were small. Then we had a chance to design a commercial turboprop for Beech Aircraft, a large corporation. This project would take all of my time for nearly a year. The airplane, called Starship, created a sensation when it was revealed to the public. Because I had done all the wing designs and the stability calculations, Beech hired me as a consultant. I spent as much as five months out of the year traveling between home, the test site in California, and the Beech factory in Wichita. I was working with engineers at both locations.

Coming Out

I really liked being with one of the engineers on the program. He had a great personality, a good sense of humor, and was quite handsome. After three months, I realized that I was in love with him. I wanted to rip his clothes off. There was no longer any doubt about it; I was gay. The object of my lust was not gay, which meant I could not talk to him about it. Being with someone I desired and having to hide it was a horrible experience. I had to watch my words and actions carefully. Did he notice that I was staring at him? Did I seem too friendly? Did he suspect something?

The suicide rate among gay teenage boys is tragically high. I understand that. The usual camaraderie among boys eventually leads to emotional or physical attraction for a companion. Having these strong feelings and having no way of dealing with them, while living in a culture which disapproves, can drive a person to despair. I was no teenager, but I remember going through severe depression and many tears because I thought that now I would be even more of an outcast. I didn't want to tell anyone. My sister Janet was very concerned, and finally I got enough courage to tell her what was going on with me. She knew a counselor at Indiana University who was gay. I made an appointment to meet with him.

Peter was a great counselor and became a good friend. The first thing he had me read was the book, *The Road Less Traveled* by M. Scott Peck. It was about relationships in general, gleaned from years working as a marriage counselor. If I was to ever find a partner, I hoped this book would help me have the right attitude. Peter introduced me to his partner, Steven. I am definitely not a bar person; fortunately, over time Peter and Steven introduced me to other gay friends. They all seemed like very nice people.

When I needed to upgrade my computer, Peter recommended a gay friend who worked for a computer company. One day Andy came by to review my requirements, and I took him out for lunch. Working on this computer upgrade we got to know each other and started dating. He was an upbeat person with an outgoing personality. I admired those traits. Three months later he asked if he could spend the night. I was ready for that. I remember that I laughed so hard I fell off the bed. I had no idea what I was doing, but I was having a great time. I finally understood what everybody was talking about. It felt normal; it felt right.

By that time I had informed my family what was going on with me. My parents even had Andy over for dinner. I had bought them a book titled, *Now That You Know: A Parent's Guide to Homosexuality*. I saw that they had the book on top of their television with two bookmarks in it. Dad had thought I was gay since I was a little boy, so he was not surprised. Mom was pleased that Dad took it so well. She had begged me not to tell him, saying that it would kill him.

I do have a funny story about this. An engineering colleague was riding his bicycle all the way from California to Maine. He stopped at my house for a few days to rest up and have some work done on his bicycle. Mom had invited me to dinner, and I asked if Jon could come. I never explained the relationship. We had dinner, and later that evening I got a phone call from my parents. Dad was on one phone and Mom on the extension. "We don't like this new guy. We like Andy better." They had assumed that I was dating Jon. It made me laugh.

Andy moved in with me a few months later. I wanted a relationship badly, and I worked very hard at this one. He seemed happy for a couple of years then started to withdraw. I tried my best to let him know that he was loved and appreciated. There came a time when he wouldn't talk to me for a couple of days. Nothing I had done precipitated this. Finally, he wrote me a note saying that I had not done anything wrong, and he was sorry for giving me the silent treatment.

A year or so later things had not improved, and I finally got the courage to confront him. "Andy, I've tried to support you in everything you wanted to do. But it's obvious that you're not happy, and I think you would be happier with another man." It was really hard to finally say what I had been feeling for a while.

He told me that we could work it out.

I had been totally integrated into his family; I had great relationships with his parents, especially his father, and his four siblings. I was there for every holiday and family birthday. I think that was the reason we stayed together for more than five years. The last year was really hard on me. We lived in the same house and slept in the same bed, but emotionally he was miles away and spent as little time at home as possible.

I grew more and more depressed. My life experience had taught me that no matter what I did or how hard I tried, I could never be loved. I desperately wanted this relationship to succeed, and I would never have ended it on my own. It was Andy who ended it. He had met a man who was twelve years younger than him, and he was in love with him. I was not surprised. I even helped him move his things into their apartment. But it hurt, really hurt. It was true; I could not be loved.

I Wanted to Die

About a month later, my dog died. I felt abandoned. I had also been betrayed at work when a new president took over at Beech and refused to honor my contract with them. I would sit outside on the deck looking at the auras around the trees crying, saying, "I hate this planet. I want to go home." I truly wanted to die.

One night I gathered the photos of my dead friends and relatives, placed them on the kitchen table, and lit a candle. I poured out my anguish, despair, and tears to them. I talked about all the hurt in my life; I begged them to take me with them. It was the lowest point of my life. Finally, I was exhausted, and asked for a sign that they had heard me. Off in the distance I heard a strange sound. I followed the sound to my bedroom. There, on my dresser, a red plastic bird—a gift from my mother—was chirping continuously. That is mechanically impossible, and I knew it. To make that bird chirp you had to turn it upside down, then right side up, after which it would chirp once. I fell to my knees and sobbed. I knew that this was a message from my spirit friends. They had heard me.

Then my body began to grant my death wish. The first episode was a gall bladder attack requiring urgent surgery.

I survived.

Four months later, I went to England to receive a prestigious award. After that, I went to Portugal to stay in a castle belonging to a friend of a friend. I was not feeling well. When I got home, I flew to Florida so my mother would not be alone on Thanksgiving. I felt very strange and had an unquenchable thirst. When I returned to Indiana, I collapsed in the driveway while shoveling snow. I didn't have the strength to get up. With considerable effort I made it to the garage and got in my car. I drove to the Elkhart Clinic to see a doctor in the immediate care facility. Noticing the white coating on my tongue and in my mouth, he checked my blood sugar with a portable machine. It was off the scale. He drew blood to get a more comprehensive test. My blood sugar level was 770. He was shocked that I actually drove myself there.

He wanted to put me in the hospital immediately and start an insulin drip. I asked him how much that would cost. The price tag: $25,000. I didn't have insurance and could not afford that. The white substance was thrush, a fungus that was thriving on the sugar in my blood. I also had a bacterial infection that was feeding on the fungus. My vision had become a total blur, except for a small area directly in front of me. He asked me if I had someone at home to look after me. I lied to him; I lived alone. He gave me some pills to reduce the blood sugar, and his home phone number. He wanted to see me again in two days. By then the blood sugar level was down to the 500s, still dangerously high. He gave me something to fight the thrush. Where the skin had been invaded by the fungus, it started to fall off. If you've ever had a blister and peeled the skin off, you know how painful the raw skin is underneath. I had that in my whole mouth. Everything hurt and tasted terrible.

I survived.

My body was still doing its best to grant my wish. The next medical event started out in a strange way. I had been using a chiropractor in Michigan who had some psychic abilities. One day as we finished, he told me that I needed to call a doctor and get a growth hormone test. I asked why. He was acting on an intense feeling, and he made me promise that I'd do that as soon as I got home. I promised.

I got home and called Dr. Rogers at the Elkhart Clinic. "I need a growth hormone test."

"John, those are for little children who aren't growing. You don't have that problem. Why do you want this test?"

"Psychic chiropractor," I said in a matter-of-fact tone.

Dr. Rogers, knowing I was not your average patient, told me to come in and have the blood drawn. Three days later he was on the phone asking me to come in and see him. The test results showed that my growth hormone levels were ten times normal. I expected him to write a prescription for some new pills. It was not so simple. He repeated the test with the same results.

Growth hormone is produced by the pituitary gland. Sometimes a tumor develops and starts cranking out lots of that hormone. It's called a pituitary adenoma. The tumor would have to be removed surgically. To figure out the best way to do this the surgeons needed an MRI using radioactive chemicals to map the area. The clinic wanted more than $2,000 for this test. I called my doctor friend, Kirt, in Chicago to see what he could do. Kirt found a clinic that would do it for $900 if I brought them a check. I agreed.

The night before the test I had my friend Sean over for dinner. Sean was a highly spiritual person who worked as a massage therapist and taught that subject at a local college. I waited until we finished before I told him. He was concerned. I climbed onto his massage table and he began by holding my head. Almost instantly I was in another place with an intense white light. It was so bright it hurt my eyes. It felt like I had risen off the table, because I couldn't feel my body.

Meanwhile Sean froze, unable to move. Tears ran down his face. He saw small arms and hands materialize out of space. The little hands reached down and touched my face. As soon as he could, he went to dry his eyes and began working on me. He said I had no reaction at all.

Then I felt myself falling. I grabbed something to hold onto, which turned out to be Sean's arm. He said I was hysterical and kept saying, "It's gone, it's gone." My face was all wet because the intensity of the light I was seeing made my eyes water.

We both had undergone very strange experiences.

The next day I drove to Chicago and had the MRI done. The tumor was gone. Follow-up tests showed that my growth hormone levels gradually had returned to normal.

This was not the end of the story. The next December I called Tim. "You wanna go to Chile and take care of sixty orphans over Christmas?"

"Yeah, I'll go."

Tim is open to pretty much any adventure with me. A classmate of mine from the seminary was now in charge of this home in Chile, which housed all these children. Some were orphans, others were there because their families could not take care of them for various reasons. The staff had some days off during the holidays, and I said I'd come to help out. It was a great experience. The children ranged from three to nineteen years old. I'd cut up the meat for the little girls when we ate. At night I'd help another lady volunteer do all the dishes. They don't have an automatic dishwasher, and you would not believe how many dirty dishes these kids could produce in a single day. But I was glad to be there helping out.

My morning routine was to come downstairs, go outside, and kneel down so that I'd be at the proper height for the kids. The little girls would come running up to me. "Tio Juan, Tio Juan." (Uncle John) They would turn their heads so I could kiss them on the cheek and give them a hug. I don't speak Spanish, but I do speak hugs. One morning a little boy stood behind the girls staring at me. Boys never want a kiss or hug, so I wondered what he was seeing. Slowly he came closer, staring intently at something just above my head. Most likely he was seeing my aura, the way I could see them around people and trees. He approached very slowly and reached out with both arms to touch the energy field he was seeing around my head. Then he lowered his arms and put his little hands on my face. I remembered Sean's vision, and chills ran through my body. The director of the center was watching this — and was amazed by what he saw. I didn't tell him about Sean's vision, but I knew that this event confirmed the supernatural character of the healing.

In my mind, I had decided that these were my final days on

earth. That's one reason I wanted to spend this time doing charitable work.

The depression was still there when I returned to my empty home.

The Vision

I had now been saved from three life threatening illnesses. Why? I got the answer much later at the Arthur Findlay College during a trance session. It was like watching a video playing in my head, complete with voice-over narration.

The spirit world needs workers who can communicate with them. Those workers are pretty rare. From their perspective, they had another person who could do this work, but this person wanted to die, and they knew that eventually I would get my wish as my body continued to fail. In the trance state I was watching a small group of spirit people as they held a meeting. They talked about my total lack of self-esteem, my disappointments in love and in business, and debated what to do about it. They had arranged for me to receive the medal from His Royal Highness Prince Philip, thinking that would snap me out of it. It didn't. They had worked through Sean to eliminate another threat to my life, leaving a vision that would serve as evidence of supernatural intervention.

I was no longer willing to trust anyone. I had been hurt too often. They discussed ways of getting me to want to continue living. The medal hadn't worked. The healing had backfired, making me appreciate the world of spirit even more and increasing my longing to return to that world. A suggestion was made that I needed to find somebody else to love, who would truly love me back. It would have to be someone that I had been with many times before in loving relationships, someone I would recognize from prior lifetimes. They went through their database. The only person currently alive who fit those requirements was a teenager living in

New England. How could they get us together? Would it work? They decided to give it a try.

It was an amazing experience to witness these things. Maybe it was just my imagination. But I have come to believe that these events, or events very much like this, really did happen.

I mentioned earlier that John Holland was going to participate in an event involving five mediums. This was the event at which Pat McKenna had singled me out. To get there, I had decided to fly to the Providence airport because it was cheaper. However, because I was going to have a three-hour layover in Chicago, I put a new hardcover book in my carry-on to read. When I got to O'Hare airport, I opened my bag and found a totally different book, *Infinite Self: 33 Steps to Reclaiming Your Inner Power* by Stuart Wilde. This was a softcover book that I had already read twice. By this time I was used to inexplicable events in my life. I decided that spirit must want me to read the book a third time.

When I arrived at Providence, I got a rental car and headed to my hotel. I had used priceline.com to find an inexpensive hotel room, which was near the Brown campus. The next morning I got up early to head to the venue where this event would be held. The ramp leading to Highway 195 was blocked off. I didn't know where the next entrance was. I drove around East Providence and found a coffee shop near Brown. I decided to go have some coffee and get directions. There was a young man sitting there reading the *New York Times,* and I asked him for directions. He invited me to sit down while he drew a map. He asked me where I was from. I told him I was from Indiana and was in town to attend a demonstration by five psychic mediums. He started asking me a lot of questions about whether these things were real. I told him about some of the events in my life and that I knew for a fact that spirits are very real. He was very curious. Then he asked me if I could recommend a book that talked about finding your own spiritual power. I started laughing. This was the very book I had with me;

now I knew why. I got his phone number, and told him I'd call after the demonstration and arrange to give him the book, which was in my hotel room.

I've already told you what happened at the demonstration. I called him on my way back to Providence and offered to pick him up because he lived on the way to my hotel. We went to my room, I gave him the book, and we started talking. We talked until three in the morning. Finally, I drove him back to the dormitory where he was staying. He had told me that his birthday was in three days. I made it a point to call him on his birthday and asked how things were going. We ended up talking again for a long time.

That's how I met Luis, who would become the great love of my life. It was May 17, 2002.

Luis

I have several friends who work with energy. Lem is a Reiki Master Teacher. Sean works with massage therapy and energy healing. Katherine is an acupuncturist. I belonged to a meditation group with some other interesting people. I asked Luis if he wanted to visit me and meet these people who would be able to provide more examples of working with energy and with the spirit world. When the semester ended at Brown, he really wanted to do this, and I got him a ticket.

My house has three floors. The lowest level is a walk-out basement overlooking a river. My concert grand piano is downstairs, along with two bedrooms that I was using as offices. The middle level has a family room, a kitchen, a formal dining room with a fireplace, a library, and the master bedroom. The top floor has two bedrooms and a large bathroom. Although I knew that Luis was gay, I recognized that he was far too cute, too young, and lived too far away for me to entertain any fantasies about a relationship with him. I picked him up at the airport and gave him his choice of the upstairs bedrooms.

During that week I introduced him to several different people who worked with Spirit. We had long discussions about his life. He had been born in Puerto Rico, the youngest of four children. The family had moved to New York City when he was still a baby. His father abandoned the family when he was about three years old and returned to Puerto Rico, where he divorced his wife and married another woman. His father had played no part in his life. His mother was stuck in New York with four children, living on welfare. She took in a female boarder to help pay the rent. This woman molested Luis. He told a friend at school about this, who informed the principal, who informed the police. The police went to his home and told his mother that she had to get rid of this woman or they'd take her children away. She was furious because she thought Luis was lying. Luis told me that she didn't speak to him for a year.

Despite his poverty and environment, Luis managed to stand out. His family moved to Providence, and he attended Classical High School, a magnet school. At the age of thirteen he joined Youth Pride, an organization to support young people with sexual orientation issues. At the age of fourteen, he joined Youth in Action, an organization devoted to helping disadvantaged youth, and wrote their HIV prevention curriculum, which is still in use. He continued his involvement with both organizations, eventually joining their boards. He received a scholarship to Brown. He worked with a small theater group as a stage manager. He worked hard to improve himself. He'd read the *New York Times* and circle all the words he didn't understand and look them up. I thought he was an amazing person.

Deep down though, he was deeply troubled and insecure. Most of his classmates at Brown came from wealthy families. They had parents who supported them; they took vacations in Europe. Luis had nothing. He was a poor, gay Hispanic kid in a white, upper class school. He felt out of place and inadequate. I understood this very well. We sat outside in the dark and just talked. I felt something really special in him. I wanted him to see himself as I saw him. He had so much potential.

A few nights later he decided to crawl into bed with me. It was not about sex; it was about continuing a deep conversation. The moment he sat down on the bed the plastic bird began chirping continuously. Luis asked me what that noise was. I pointed to the red plastic bird on the dresser across the room.

"How did you turn it on?"

"I didn't turn it on."

"How do you make it stop?"

"I can't make it stop." All this time I was laughing. I knew this was a message from my spirit friends. Finally I told him that if he wanted it to stop, he'd have to ask it.

"Hey bird. Be quiet."

The bird stopped chirping. I thought this was hilarious. Luis would say something, and the bird would answer him. I just kept laughing. This went on for a while.

Finally, I said, "Okay, bird. I know you're happy, but Luis is tired and needs his sleep." The bird stopped chirping and remained silent for the rest of the night. This was the first time Luis had witnessed a real miracle, and it made a deep impression on him.

At the end of the week, it was time for him to return to Providence. He looked at me and said, "I'm not tired of you yet."

I had to smile.

The summer was hard on him. He was sliding deeper into depression. He wanted more money; he was tired of being poor. He made some questionable friends and got into drugs and raves. I could understand it. All his friends had cars and money to go on nice vacations. He was stuck on a bus going across town to work for minimum wage. What was the point? He dropped out of school. We continued talking on the phone and via email. I kept encouraging him because I knew there was so much potential in him. When he would put himself down, I'd counter with some of the great things he had accomplished.

If this was the spirit world's plan, it was working. I became more concerned with Luis than with my own problems. I wanted to protect him, but I also knew that when he volunteered for this lifetime, he chose to face difficult situations in order to overcome them. Sometimes he'd tell me things that made me cringe. One night he was robbed at knifepoint, for example. I sent him crystals that were supposed to have protective powers. Some choices he made scared me. But I felt that if I tried to rescue him, he'd never face the challenges he was fated to face. So I'd wait for him to fail, then I'd pick him up and reassure him. I sent him books about Kabbalah, which he found helpful and interesting.

A Special Trip

I owned a couple of timeshare weeks on Kauai, and I wanted to take him there. I said "Okay, Spirit, if you want this to happen, you'll have to provide the means." A couple of weeks later I got a phone call from Frank and Frieda. They were an older couple who drove to Canada every three months to buy their prescription drugs. At that time, they would save more than $1,000 buying the same pills in Canada rather than the states. They asked if I wanted to ride along. I had nothing going on, and I went with them. On the way there they told me about a casino in Windsor at which you could get a free lunch by signing up for their free player's card. This sounded good to me. After they got their medicine, we went to the casino. We got our lunches and decided to play for a while. I played a 25-cent machine and was up $40. I decided to try a different machine. I walked around the floor just looking. Every time I passed a certain machine, called Wheel of Fortune, I stopped and stared at it. Finally, I decided to play this machine. On the first spin I won $400. I kept winning and winning, drawing a small crowd. Finally, the machine ran out of coins. The staff waited a long while before coming to refill it. At last they came, and the machine continued to spit out my winnings. In the end, I had several buckets of coins, and they were very heavy. I took them to the cashier's booth, and they counted them. I had won $7,550!

I asked Luis when he wanted to go to Hawaii. He thought it would be nice to be there for our birthdays. His is May 20 and mine is May 25. I bought first-class tickets for us. We both flew to Cincinnati and met up there. On the airplane, Luis rested his head on my shoulder and fell asleep. I had always been self-conscious, and I worried about what the flight attendants would think. Eventually, Luis taught me not to be afraid of what other people thought. Whenever we were waiting for an airplane, he would put his head on my shoulder. Some people would see this and smile. Some would look at us then jerk their heads away. He even kissed me on the lips once in a public store. After a while I came to feel that we had the right to be ourselves, and if other people had a problem with that, it was their problem.

We stayed for one night on Waikiki Beach because we arrived too late to fly to another island. As he was unpacking, he told me that he had seen so many wonderful things happen to me, and he wondered if Spirit would let him experience similar kinds of things.

"Have you asked?"

"What do you mean?"

"They can't interfere with your life unless you give them permission."

"Okay, Spirit," he said. "I've seen the things that have happened to John. I would like those kinds of things to happen to me." He looked at me. "Was that okay?"

I told him it was good enough.

The next morning he woke up and went outside on the tiny deck to enjoy the sunshine and blue sky. I was in the bathroom when I heard him holler. When I went to look he was running towards me.

"What happened?"

"Something fell out of the sky and hit me in the legs."

"What was it?"

"I don't know; I ran."

We went outside and picked it up. It was a nice Hawaiian shirt in his size.

"You asked," I said, laughing.

Later we walked down the street to get some breakfast. A man stopped us on the street. "Do you guys always smile like that?"

"Well, now that we're here," I said. "We're all smiles."

"I want you guys to know that your smiles make the trees smile, and the birds smile, and the fish smile. So keep smiling."

I liked that sentiment. We opened the door to the restaurant and glanced behind us. There was no one on the street.

We took a flight to Kona on the Big Island, where we stayed for a week. I wanted to show him the active volcano there. We visited several *heiaus* (Hawaiian temples) around the island, where we would stop and meditate. One day I told him that I wanted to introduce him to a goddess. He said that he'd better wear his good shirt. Luis had a terrific sense of humor and kept me laughing much of the time. We drove through Volcanoes National Park, and then I parked the car and we hiked out over the lava to a place called Halemaumau. This is the location where Pele, the Volcano Goddess, was said to live. Luis bent down to feel steam coming out of the ground. At that instant I saw a bright violet light coming out of the ground and illuminating him. I didn't know if it was physical or a vision, so I grabbed my camera and took a picture of it. It was real. To me it meant that spiritual powers greater than me thought he was very special too.

I like doing pencil drawings. Luis said that he couldn't draw, but I knew that wasn't true. So we stopped at an art store in Hilo, and I bought him some pencils and drawing paper. Later back at our condo, I gave him some exercises designed to teach him that drawing is about seeing in a different way. He caught on right away. A year later he told me he thought he had been an artist in a previous lifetime.

The resort offered ukulele lessons, and Luis signed up. He was really good at it. I secretly bought him a ukulele for his birthday.

He went paragliding on his birthday. I watched him hanging from the parachute screaming at the top of his lungs, "I'm the king of the world!"

That night we went to a Japanese restaurant at the Hilton Waikoloa Village. Outside was a full size statue featuring four bronze horses pulling a bronze cart that had two life-sized bronze statues sitting in it. Luis ran over and climbed into the cart, putting his arm around one of the statues, and pretended to be a tour guide. Once again he made me laugh. We had a wonderful sushi dinner and some excellent wine. I toasted his birthday. He was twenty years old.

Then we flew to Kauai and stayed at the resort where I owned a timeshare. I had been there every year for more than ten years and knew the island well. Like the condo in Kona, it was a two bedroom, two-bath unit. The master bedroom faces the ocean, and the entire wall is glass, which can be left open since the openings are covered by screens. I loved to hear the waves crashing at night, and so did he, so we slept in the big king bed.

I woke up the next morning face down on the pillow. Luis reached over and gently began stroking my back. His touch was so soft, so gentle, so loving. I burst into tears. All the hurt and pain in my life gushed out. He had managed to break through all my defenses, and all the things I had been holding inside came rushing out. I was crying so hard that I had trouble breathing. I'm sure he was frightened, but I couldn't stop. I was releasing all that pain. Finally, I was able to look at him.

"Are you okay?" he asked.

"I've never been better in my whole life" I replied, with tears running down my face. We hugged, then kissed, and made love for the first time. I joked with him. "I've been in love with your soul for a long time, but your body isn't so bad either." We laughed.

We hiked up to the top of the Na Pali lookout, where there is a wonderful view down a valley towards the ocean, and sat there to meditate. We went to see a waterfall. After everyone else had left, a rainbow formed in the mist. Then a large white bird with a long streaming tail that looked like ribbons began playing with the waterfall. Another bird joined, then a third. They would swoop down, climb back up, and circle as though they were having a good time. I noticed that they never flapped their wings. Being quite familiar with the laws of lift, I thought this was very strange.

We watched them for a while then looked at each other. We said simultaneously, "I don't think those are birds." We laughed at having said the same thing at the same time. Later Luis found a *kahuna* (Hawaiian holy man) and described the birds.

"Those aren't birds. Those are spirits."

It confirmed what we suspected already.

Luis took a lot of photos, and by the end of the day the battery was dead. We came to a beautiful place called The Cathedral, which is supposed to have great spiritual power. He was sad that he didn't have enough battery power to take a picture. He decided to try once more, and incredibly the battery was showing a full charge. He ran that camera for another day and a half without needing to recharge the battery. Our group in Egypt had a similar experience in the Temple of Hathor. Everyone who had a battery-operated camera found that their batteries had fully recharged inside the temple.

Luis took me out to dinner for *my* birthday and gave me a video of Israel Kamakawiwo'ole, a famous Hawaiian singer, as a present.

It was time to leave. We flew back to Honolulu, where we faced a seven-hour layover. I decided we should rent a car and go for a ride. We took the shuttle to Avis, and found a huge line there waiting to rent a car. More people poured in behind us. A man came over to us, and told us to follow him. He lifted the rope so we could get by, took us to his private office and said, "What can I do for you two?" I explained that we needed a car for a few hours. He replied, "Well, I'm going to do this just because I can. You can have a new convertible for $10." We just looked at each other. Pretty soon we were putting the top down on our nice new car. Khonsu had blessed me. Pele had blessed Luis. Whatever was happening, it was a good thing.

We did a little sightseeing then drove to the Byodo-In Temple, one of my favorite places. It is the re-creation of the original Byodo-In Temple in Japan, and it is gorgeous. We lit incense in front of the statue of the Buddha and stayed to meditate a while. I told Luis that I wanted to be cremated, and I wanted my ashes placed in this temple. I made him promise to do that for me.

Sushi was Luis' favorite food. I remembered a good sushi restaurant in Waikiki, so we decided to go there for dinner. It was four P.M., and the restaurant didn't open until five. We walked down to the International Market Place, a big tourist trap with lots of little stores winding indoors for about a block. It's a fun place. By the time we got to the end of it, it was a quarter to five. I saw an alley nearby that I thought would take us back more quickly. We started walking down the alley. Sitting there was a large Hawaiian lady and a table full of loose flowers. The smell was intoxicating. I walked up to her and commented that I had never seen such nice flowers.

"You take some home."

I explained that we were flying back to the mainland in a few hours, and they wouldn't keep.

"No money—free," she replied. She took out a needle and thread, and sewed a beautiful lei, which she handed to Luis. "You put on him."

We faced each other, and Luis hung the lei around my neck. Then she made another one which she gave to me. "Now you put on him."

I hung the lei around his neck. This was a very emotional experience, almost like a marriage ceremony. We offered to pay for them, but she would not accept anything. We thanked her again and continued down the alley. A little further down there was a jog to the right that I thought would lead to the other side. But it was a dead end. We turned around, and there was no lady, no table, and no flowers.

Luis kept that lei until it fell apart—to remind him that angels are real. We had done everything we wanted to do, never counting how much money we had left. When I got on the plane to return home, I had one dollar remaining. Spirit knew exactly how much money I'd need on this trip.

Our Trip to Italy

Luis headed back to Providence, and I returned to Elkhart. A couple of days later I got a card from him. "I am so happy to have found you again in this lifetime," he wrote. We had never talked about it, but I was positive that we had been together before.

With a much more positive attitude Luis decided to go back to school. He had a couple of incomplete grades because he had not turned in his final projects. I helped him reconstruct those papers so that he could get a grade for those classes. He changed his major from business to management of non-profit organizations. He wanted to devote his life towards helping the disadvantaged. He would sometimes call me while walking to class and just say, "I love you. I love you. I love you," then hang up.

Luis had joined me for the weekend with John Holland and also for the group session at Pat McKenna's house. His experience with energy and working with Spirit made a huge impression on him. He encouraged me to develop my psychic and mediumistic talents and was excited that I'd be going to the Arthur Findlay College, wanting to know everything that happened there. For Valentine's Day I sent him a big box filled with every kind of candy I could find, along with a cute video, "Bambi," because he had similar beautiful brown eyes. We kept in touch mostly by instant messaging.

I could also sense when he was having a rough time. Sometimes he'd fall into depression and wouldn't leave his room for a couple of days. Somehow I knew this, and I was always there reminding him how special he was and how loved he was. I took the photo of him being lit by a violet light coming from the ground and made it into a wall hanging. I wrote a verse on it: "In the quiet of this day may you know the greatness of your soul, and how much you are truly loved." He hung it above his desk as a reminder.

I would occasionally fly to Providence to see him, and when he had a break, he'd come here. We spent the next Christmas in Hawaii on the island of Molokai. We spent the following Christmas on a cruise in the Caribbean. The love just kept growing stronger. I didn't know that a human being could feel such joy.

He was interested in organic farming, and he had found an organization that paired volunteers with organic farmers. Volunteers would get room and board in exchange for their labor. He wanted to go to Italy and carefully selected two organic farms that had no electricity. He spent the summer of 2005 living with me before flying to Italy.

The plan was that he'd spend one week at each of the farms, and then I'd fly over and we'd travel around Italy together for two weeks. I rented a car in Pisa, and we basically drove all over the country. We had studied Italian together that summer, and he was pretty fluent in it by the time I arrived. Italy is a beautiful country with lots of history. Our favorite day was spent driving through the vineyards of Tuscany. Unfortunately, I was robbed by a highly skilled pickpocket in Rome, which did set us back a while.

After two weeks we flew back through Munich and Chicago. He had to return to Providence for his last year in college. He was graduating that spring, and he was looking forward to having his family and me there for that occasion.

Although we had always spent Christmas together, that year he found a cheap flight to California, where he could spend time with friends and classmates. I told him that it was okay with me, so he went. Because it was cold and wet in California at the time, he and a friend decided to take a bus into Mexico, where it was warmer. He was on the phone with me constantly while in California, but his cell phone didn't work in Mexico. Instead, he wrote daily emails. I got two emails from him on January 11. They were starting their trip back to California the next day, and he had so much to tell me.

Tragedy Strikes

On the morning of January 12, 2006, he decided to go for a swim in the ocean before leaving. He disappeared. I didn't know about it for two days until I got an email from one of his friends at Brown, who found out from classmates in California. His body was recovered by fishermen four days later. They identified him by his necklace, which I had made for his birthday. I had carved the Hawaiian petroglyph called Honu, the sea turtle, as its center-piece. Its back was made from polished moldavite. He loved that necklace and would never take it off. Luis was twenty-two years old.

I disintegrated. I called Sean and couldn't even speak. I just cried into the phone. He came over, but all I could do was cry. No words can describe my despair. I had not only lost the most important person in my life, but I was now an outsider. I had no authority to call the U.S. Embassy in Mexico to find out what was going on. I had no authority to decide what to do with his body. I had never met his mother. I started doing crazy things, like putting dirty clothes in the dishwasher. I called my friend Tim and told him I was scared because I was losing my mind. Tim drove down from Chicago to stay with me. I talked to Luis' friends at Brown and learned that they were shipping his body back to Providence. Since the coffin would be sealed, I decided to print up some large photos of him to display at the funeral home. I cried all the way to Providence, rented a car, and drove to his brother's house, where his mother was staying. She greeted me at the door. We sat down and talked. She knew that Luis had spent a lot of time away from home, and she usually knew where he went, but she never knew that it was always with the same person. She was very kind to me.

I stayed in Luis' room at the co-op where he lived. The students there were understanding and compassionate. I was impressed with them. When the time came, we went to the funeral home early so I could put up the photos on a bulletin board. Only his family was there. I took a deep breath and went inside the main room. I hugged his coffin and cried for a long time. The grief was unbearable. The photo above his coffin was taken on our Christmas cruise and showed Luis wearing a tuxedo. I had also brought the last drawing I made of him as he was meditating. They put that on an easel near the front of the room. I finally met his other sisters and his brother. I was shocked that his father came. He had had nothing to do with Luis, but his sisters had insisted that he come.

Because of his involvement with youth and theater, more than a hundred people came to pay their respects. His friends would break down, come over to me, and we would hug and cry together. The mayor came. The president of Brown came. They went over to the family and expressed their sorrow.

I sat there looking at his father. All these people were telling him how great his son was. I hoped that he felt really stupid, because he didn't even know his son. Finally, I went over to him and shook his hand. I decided that without him Luis would not exist and for that one act I should be grateful to him.

His brother had given Luis a hard time, constantly putting him down for being gay. I knew all those stories. His wife came over to me and told me that her husband had something to say to me. I took a deep breath and went over to him. He hugged me so hard I could barely breathe. He started wailing in a loud voice, thanking me for taking care of his little brother. People were staring at us because he was crying so loudly. I decided to forgive him for the way he had treated Luis.

Then I saw a mail carrier in the back of the room. He didn't know anyone and was standing all alone. I went over to him, shook his hand, and thanked him for coming. He told me that of all the people he had met on his mail route, he always hoped he would see Luis, because he made him laugh, and he made him feel special. It touched me deeply. How many of us make such an impression that our mail carriers come to mourn us?

The next day there was a private ceremony for the family at the chapel at Brown. His mother made sure I sat with the family. God bless her for that. I had shown her photos of the Byodo-In Temple in Hawaii, and I asked if I could take his ashes there. She decided to divide the ashes with me. They were waiting for the rest of his belongings to come back from Mexico. I really wanted the necklace back because it meant so much to him, but I had to fly back to Indiana.

Climbing Out of a Black Hole

I kept asking Luis to let me know that he was okay. For several days nothing happened, and in my depression I stopped expecting anything. One night I walked into my bedroom and sat down on the end of the bed. "Honey, I really need a hug."

The bird chirped! He had figured out how to control the bird. The next time I walked into my bedroom the bird chirped continuously. I cried, this time out of joy. I knew he was okay and was still connected to me.

A day or two later I got a phone call from Nancy Garber. She is a medium whom I had met when I went to Boston to work with Glyn Edwards. I had emailed her about Luis even though she had never met him. She was calling from Hawaii, where she was on vacation. She told me she had a faint link that she thought was Luis. She said he was holding his diploma and jumping up and down. I learned later that Brown had awarded his degree posthumously. She talked about him buying new shoes and needing to get inserts for them. True. She'd lose him—and then get him back. She told me things that only he and I knew. I knew she had linked to him, and it confirmed that he was okay. I was so grateful to Nancy for calling me.

The only thing that came back from Mexico was a shirt and some jeans. I was disappointed. I flew back to Providence because I could not imagine shipping his ashes through the mail. I brought his mother 120 photos of him taken over the years that we knew each other. I explained each one and where it was taken. Then I received a container with his ashes. I held them to my heart and fought off the tears. I flew back the same day. I cannot describe what it felt like to hold this little container knowing that this was all that was left of the person I loved so very much. I made a little shrine in my bedroom next to the plastic bird and placed the ashes there until I could take them to Hawaii.

I had already booked two courses at Stansted, beginning in March—two months after his death—and I really wanted to go. His best friend was Ayla, who had graduated from Brown and was in Israel working with an Arab-Israeli nonprofit organization. She was devastated and was bearing her grief alone in a foreign country. I wanted to fly to Israel and spend some time with her then fly to London from there. The problem was financial. I had not been able to work since Luis died—I just couldn't focus. My expenses were up. I had spent a lot of money going back and forth to Providence, so I asked Spirit for help.

Years before I had designed a wing for a company in Oregon, for which I was paid a tiny royalty ($15) on each airplane. One day I got a letter from them, saying that they had audited the books and decided that they owed me $4,530. They asked me to send them an invoice. I knew that there was no way they had sold that many airplanes, so definitely Spirit was at work. I faxed the invoice and deposited the check when it came. It was more than I needed.

I picked up Ayla in Tel Aviv, and we drove north along the Mediterranean coast to Haifa, then east until we arrived at a horse ranch overlooking the Sea of Galilee where I had booked a cabin for us. I had brought her some of Luis' clothes and a large stack of photos. We shared many memories and tears. It helped both of us. We drove back along the river Jordan, while the scenery changed from lush green to dry desert as we went south. At Jericho we turned back west, driving through Jerusalem and back to Tel Aviv. Then I flew to London.

I had been talking to Luis every day since his death. I felt his presence around me. I kept telling him that I was going to be in a house full of mediums and that if he didn't come through every day, he'd never hear the end of it when I crossed over!

I was assigned to Simone Key as I hoped. At the first session on the first day, she asked us to pair up with someone we didn't know. We were to exchange readings, and Simone would stop and listen in for a while in order to gauge our abilities. I paired up with an English man named Andy. Andy wanted to go first. He started by describing Luis in detail, then he blushed dark red. "It's okay, Andy, just say it." He told me that he had an overwhelming urge to come over and kiss me. I cried.

I was having a really hard time controlling my grief. Whenever we would do meditation, tears would run down my face even though I wasn't crying. A lady sitting in front of me during meditation turned around and asked if I was okay. She had picked up on the sadness. My Irish roommate told me that I cried all night long, even though I was asleep. My pillow would be soaking wet every morning.

The next night three advanced students were demonstrating. A Belgian medium, Isabelle, immediately pointed at me and said that she had my father. I had never met Isabelle before, and she didn't know anything about me. She said that Dad was here to give me strength because of the stress I was going through. She said he was with someone name Luisa. I told her I thought the name was Luis. She cut me off saying that it didn't matter, and she never mentioned it again, which I found upsetting. After the demonstration was over, she pulled me into a side room and told me the name was really Luis, but she was fighting back tears on the platform and she just couldn't break down in public. She told me that he loved me and is always with me. Luis was angry at himself for going swimming. He said that a big wave got him and that he didn't suffer.

I booked a private sitting with Simone, my tutor. She began by telling me that an amazing power was working with me, that in my teenage years I had felt second class, but that I was now coming into my own. Then she said a man was here—"a beautiful man, who doesn't have a bad bone in his body. He was generous, kind and loving, and he couldn't believe the life you've lived and what people did to you." She told me that Luis was glad that he got through to me so quickly, and Simone added that he was referring to someone else's help, not hers. I knew that Luis was talking about Nancy. Simone saw a vision of me going through his things, holding his jacket, and wanting to smell him. I broke down. I had done that very thing. She said he believed in the power of love, he knew his passing happened in such a disturbing way, but he wanted me to know it was quick and he didn't suffer. She wanted to know if this happened in a boating accident because it felt like he fell out of something into the water. Luis said that he was pleased that I got along so well with his mother because she could have shut me out completely. He said that we had a wonderful relationship; he had never stopped loving me, and I had never stopped loving him. He knew this was the hardest time in my life, and that the funeral was nearly impossible for me. He thanked me for deciding to plant a tree in my back yard in his memory, and he correctly described the tree. He thanked me for being so kind to him when nobody else was—and for helping him to understand who he is. He had worked through many issues with me. He said that I had taught him how to love, and this was the greatest gift I could have ever given him.

Simone also gave me very specific information, which mediums call evidence. She talked about how we had watched science fiction together. Luis and I had watched Star Trek every day. She talked about his secret chocolate eating. He hid the chocolates I sent him for Valentine's Day because his housemates kept eating them. He loved that we chose our clothes together. She talked about the back of his head. I used to trim it because he didn't like it long. Then she asked if we had an issue with pillows. I was astounded by that. Luis hated the pillows on my bed, so we went to Bed Bath & Beyond and spent half an hour squeezing pillows, and pressing them against our heads. In the end we bought four new pillows, which cost almost $300. How could she possibly know that?

When the reading was over, I felt that I truly had touched him again. The details she provided were totally accurate. But hearing all those things made me miss him even more.

My next course was with Simon James. At the opening event, he told us that he wants us to be alive. "There is no point in being able to talk to the dead if we can't talk to the living. We know that life continues. So why are we not afraid of death, but afraid of life?" It made me stop and think. I was having a terrible time facing life without Luis.

The next day one of the other tutors was ill, and Simon told her group to join ours. He told us to pair up with someone we didn't know. I asked the lady next to me if she wanted to work with me. We pulled our chairs away from the group. But another lady came to me and also wanted to work with me. She wouldn't take no for an answer, and she pulled up a third chair. I could see that she had something important to say. However, Simon came over to her and said that another lady didn't have a partner, and she had to go and pair with her.

We broke for tea, and afterwards we were told to pair up again. I went over to this lady, whose name was Lynne. She belonged to the other group, and I had never met her before. She sat down and immediately blurted out, "I have your partner here. And the love … the love … the love between you two. It feels like my chest has been torn open and my heart has been ripped out." Lynne was truly feeling the intense pain of this tragedy, and I ended up comforting her. Luis was exploring his new world and finding lots of things to do. He said he was glad that he went first, because he couldn't have faced life without me. I thanked Lynne for that. Afterwards, I wondered whether I could face life without him.

I had also booked a private sitting with Simon James. Although I had been in his group before, he knew nothing about my relationship or anything about Luis. He told me that he had been seeing dolphins around me all week. Luis and I had gone swimming with dolphins. He said that this person had been working on papers and studying for exams; that he had passed away after he hit his head and blacked out, losing consciousness; and that he didn't suffer. Simon then got an image of big waves and a strong undertow. He said this was a freak accident, that ninety-nine times out of a hundred, it wouldn't have happened. He even got the name Alyssa, which is Ayla's real name. He said that Luis was in a cocoon of restfulness and peace, that he got an overwhelming sense of peace with him. He said that the way we met was very unusual, that we could never have planned it. Luis encouraged me to continue, not to give up. He wanted me to do this work of mediumship. Once again, I felt that I had touched Luis in a special way.

One of the most advanced members of our group was a lady named Leela. Even though we are forbidden to give readings outside of class, we borrowed a tape recorder from a tutor so that I could record her illicit reading. She described him as my partner, with a slim, beautiful face and beautiful eyes. He sent so much love, trying to take the tears back. She asked if he had gone surfing. He got tipped up and all tangled up. She felt crushing in her lungs, which she said was a horrible sensation. I cringed. She said that we were the best thing that ever happened to each other. She could see me clutching his photo to my chest and crying. She saw me holding his shirt, clinging to it, and kissing it. She mentioned the card that he sent me. I had been reading it over and over. She said to put the card away. I said, "No." Then she said he had a special thing around his neck, and she saw him kissing it. He said they had taken it off him, and he wanted me to have it. Finally, she brought through my father. He said that he was sorry for treating me the way he did. He said he's sending me all this love now, because he didn't when he was on the earth plane. Once again, I felt so grateful for this reunion with Luis.

When it was time to return home, I had heard from Luis every day. I had more proof than I could have ever hoped for that it was really him. Yet I kept wanting more and more. Everything I had heard had still not quieted the longing within me.

Return to Hawaii

Luis had a Facebook page, and I had asked his friends at Brown to spread the word that I wanted them to post short messages saying how much Luis had meant to them. I printed them all out. The friends he had made here in Indiana also wrote notes to him. I wrote a long letter and printed up some photographs of us together. I bought a large urn, and ordered a name plate for it. I also bought a beautiful hand-blown glass bottle. I packed everything except his ashes in my suitcase. I hand-carried his ashes with me—and flew to Hawaii.

In my hotel room, I put his ashes into the large bottle and placed the bottle in the urn, which left a little space around it. I took all these notes and messages and wrapped them around the bottle containing his ashes. There were more than a hundred of them. I put in some small items that friends had sent, put my letter in, and the photos. I wanted Luis to always be surrounded by love.

The next morning I drove to the Byodo-In Temple. I had already made an appointment with them. Since I had purchased a niche for one urn, I had to buy a larger one so that eventually two urns could be placed in it. The Buddhist bishop greeted me. I placed the urn on the altar in front of the statue of the Buddha and lit some incense. The bishop chanted some sutras, then we went into the room behind the statue. He opened a glass case, and I placed the urn and a photograph of Luis with his big smile inside. We blessed it with incense, and the bishop replaced the glass covering the case. I stayed a while to meditate. I had asked Luis to bring my ashes here, never imagining that it would be the other way around. It was comforting to know that someday my ashes will rest beside his. I went back to the hotel and sat outside on the tiny deck. A white dove flew over and sat at my feet, looking at me.

Returning to Stansted

I returned to Stansted in October, 2008, for a course with Mavis. We focused on trance, and she shared her wealth of experience with us. She encouraged us to talk to the spirits after we finished a reading, asking them how we could have done better. She reminded us that our clients are in the spirit world, and we work for them regardless of what the living person in front of us thinks. It was a fresh perspective, which has served me well. There was a tutor working that week whom I had never met before. I booked a private sitting with Colin Bates. It's much easier if the medium knows nothing about the person. I also booked another sitting with Sharon, who was a last-minute substitute for a sick tutor. I did not know her either.

My meeting with Sharon came first. She started by saying that a gentleman was coming in, and he wanted to hold my hand. She said that we used to sit together, holding hands. "Soulmates. Absolutely. Soulmates." She said that we used to laugh, and plan meals, and that he liked wine, not beer. He was reading a lot trying to learn things. But he felt a lot of frustration, because he felt so inadequate. She told me, "You made him feel whole. You made him feel good." For that he couldn't thank me enough. She said that we didn't have a long time together, that we had found each other, that we had this happiness, that finally we could have time together, but now it was gone. Sharon said that although it was a short time, "it was so amazing and so fantastic, and there are a lot of people who never get that in a whole lifetime."

Sharon said he didn't get a lot of love in his life; he didn't have a really good time in his life. He felt so inadequate; he felt that he was no good. "You gave him a new lease on life. He came from nothing; he had nothing. But for the first time in his life, he felt loved. I feel inadequate to tell you how much he loved you, John. I don't know how to put this in words. You brought a special time to someone's life."

Sharon said that how we met wasn't normal. She said that sometime in his life he was bossed around and made to do things he didn't want to do. I knew about that. She said there was something strange about his passing, something wasn't right. She also told me that I didn't find out right away and that it really hurt not to know what was happening.

"Life has been hard for you," Sharon said to me. "Love has been the bane of your life, do you understand that? You've carried a lot of pain from love. It's been such a terrible journey for you, then you find something so wonderful, then it's gone. This journey is so hard and so difficult. It's so heavy. I want to take this off, it's so heavy."

She ended by telling me that I have a photo of him by my bed, and I say good night and good morning to him, and even ask him questions. She wanted me to know how much he loves that, that he hears me, that he is there with me.

Then it was time for my private sitting with Colin. He had never met me and knew nothing about me. He got a link almost instantly and began speaking quickly: "I have a very strong independent mind here, and a very strong independent person. Also, this was not a person who opened their hearts easily to anyone ... I'm starting to feel the smile and the energy, and there is a terrific smile here, and you have photographs of the smile, you have photographs of the face and the head and this tremendous smile.

"I know that there was a part of his life that was very wild, so full of people and things, but I want to say that the life you had together was very different, but it was the life that he wanted. It was the life that he'd always wanted ... I have tremendous memories of sitting down or laying down, and just simply being ... There were times upon a couch, a big couch, when I want to lay against you and slop, with you and over you, and I'm still doing it."

Colin continued: "And laughter, and it was a high-pitched laughter, and it's an infectious laughter, and it's almost as if there were so many private things between the two of you that really anybody who was looking on would not understand or even get between the two of you. The eyes are so full of love, and of energy, and of laughter.

"I have to say, it's like I went through many changes of life, and also I went through many changes of life with you as well. There were parts of life that he didn't like, because there's something here where he wasn't happy, and this relates to a past part of his life. But I know also that you supported me through a time of great transition and turmoil in my life. And for that, it's like you gave me life.

And for that there is a tremendous sense here of gratitude, but also it was right. Almost as if everything that you did, and everything that you experienced together was something that was so intimate that it didn't involve anyone else. And I have to say that to you. And he's just saying 'nobody understood. Nobody understood.' And he says, 'ask me if I was bothered,' and I know he wasn't."

Colin said, "I have to talk to you a little bit about the passing, because I know it's evidential. Immediately here I am conscious of the passing happening so quickly that I wasn't aware of it. There is this feeling here of not being able to control what was taking place. I know that the passing would have been very, very quick. It's almost as if something carried me away. So I know that it was totally an accidental passing to the spirit world. This essence of sadness is the fact that he's no longer here. It's here with you, but it's also there within the spirit world. I feel it's more of a reflection upon 'I can't believe this.'

"But I have to say to you that you gave to him something that he had very seldom touched in his life, if ever, and I also have to say to you that in some way you saved his life."

"And he saved mine," I said, "so that's true."

"And that is true, absolutely," Colin said. "So I know in a sense that he will always be there with you. But it's, ohhh. ... But it's, ohhh. ... It's just the heart and the energy and the smile. Because time will change and life will move, but the essence of what I felt here for you I know will remain constant. The partner you've been with—I mean, it's devastation. I can't put flowery words before you, because it's not what it is. What is important more than anything is that no one can touch what you had. From that perspective the love that you have for each other is as strong as the day that it became love. And truly that will never change for you."

He continued, "I want just to exist at the moment, and just to really try and get that strength moving and growing again, and in a way start to utilize that and then allow it to take you where it will take you. You have many years of your life—and I'm not saying that to depress you. But in a way it is to talk about the many experiences you still have, that will be in a different way from those that you've already had. And so I think in some way, the future is yet to be written. "

I was numb. By far this was the most profound reading I'd ever had. Colin had been able to feel Luis, to feel his heart, in a way that no one else had. He was able to perceive what the relationship really meant to both of us. If we had not found each other, we would both be dead. The feeling in the room was intense. Twice Colin was so overcome that he could only sigh. Lynne was the only other person who had felt that much pain.

Colin's reading finally satisfied my heart. I didn't need more validations or evidence. There really was nothing more anyone could ever say. It taught me a great lesson. I thought that getting a name or an obscure event, like the pillow episode, was the highest level of mediumship. Colin showed me that being able to truly *feel* the person, to *know* their emotions, was far more important. It changed the way I approach my own mediumship. I have to smile when I remember Colin saying that he didn't want to depress me but that I'd have a long life.

Living with His Presence

Like many other people who've lost the most important person in their life, I have never gotten over it—and probably never will. But as time goes by I've adjusted to it. Luis taught me that in spite of all the negatives in my life, I truly can be loved.

I can also say that without hearing from him so often through the miracle of mediumship, I doubt if I could have ever climbed out of the black hole of grief that had swallowed me. No amount of grief therapy can equal hearing the words and feelings of your loved ones. Having gone through this myself, I became more committed to helping others who are also grieving.

Luis continues to demonstrate his presence. I dream about him and wake up crying. The plastic bird chirps at me. It is his way of showing me that he's still around. I have a three-bulb light fixture above my kitchen table. One of the lamps does not light, because there is no power to that socket, and it's too much trouble to fix. One night I was watching the movie, *Dreamgirls,* and one of the songs really got to me. The tears started forming. Suddenly that light came on. It was his way of showing that he's still here. Spirits are pure energy, and they can do things like turn on lights, even when there is no power. It has never come on since.

A couple of times I've felt the bed move as though he had just climbed in. The first time it startled me, but then I figured out what it was. When he embraces me, I get a powerful tingling sensation from head to foot.

I bought a used car in Peoria, Illinois. I had taken a train to Chicago, and a friend drove me to Peoria from there. It was evening before I started the long drive home, and I talked to Luis on the way. The next morning I got an email from my medium friend Isabelle in Belgium. She told me that Luis woke her up and told her to write me to say that he had been riding in the car with me the day before. I cried again for the first time in a long time.

On my recent trip back to England I had a private sitting with another tutor, Maureen, who did not know me. She got Luis right away. Her comment was that we were like lost sheep; when we found each other, we knew that we had been together before many times and that this reunion would last forever. We had made a pact before we incarnated, that I would find him late in life, and we would not have a lot of time together. She said that without him I would not be doing this work, and so my relationship to the spirit world was the child of both of us. She told me that I wanted to grow old and die to be with him again but that I have a lot of work yet to accomplish. She knew that I was writing a book and encouraged me to finish it. The idea that Luis and I had agreed to what would happen ahead of time made me look at this life in a new way. I have to prove that I can go on without him; when my job is done, we will be together again.

Several years earlier I had restored an older Jaguar convertible, and Luis often drove that car. It was turning cold, and I decided it was time to wash the car and put up the top for the winter. I noticed something black and white in the back, which had never been there before. I picked it up and discovered that it was one of Luis' shirts. I had been listening to the CD of my reading with Maureen over and over, thinking about my pre-birth agreement with Luis. I'm positive that finding his shirt was his way of demonstrating the truth of this and proving that he's still with me.

Some people want to know if I can link with him directly. The problem with doing that is that it's very hard to know if it's really coming from him or from my own memories. I often wake up with a song playing in my head, which I notice after a while. Sometimes I have to research the lyrics. They are always messages of love. So he uses this technique to communicate with me.

He was my best teacher, and I am so blessed to have found him. Even though the relationship lasted less than four years, I realize that very few people have experienced a love so intense and profound. I will spend the rest of my life missing him. But I know that he's okay and that he'll always be with me. We will have other lifetimes to share.

On this journey I have experienced the bliss of love and the horror of loss. I've met hundreds of people who are alive in another plane of existence. I have learned a lot about the spirit world from them.

I hope that in sharing my experiences you have come to understand these truths: you are immortal, the spirit world is very real, and love never dies.

I found a poem in a Jewish prayer book that expresses my sentiments better than I ever could. It says

It is a fearful thing to love what death can touch.
A fearful thing to love, hope, dream: to be –
To be and oh! To lose.

A thing for fools this, and a holy thing,
A holy thing to love.

For your life has lived in me,
Your laugh once lifted me,
Your word was gift to me.

To remember this brings a painful joy.
'Tis a human thing, love,
A holy thing.
To love
What death has touched.

My Aeronautical Career.

IT'S HARD TO SAY WHERE my interest in airplanes came from. My father enlisted in the Army Air Corps and was a bombardier in World War II, but he never encouraged my interest in airplanes. As a kid in the 1950s, I'd be paid 50 cents per week to mow the lawn and do other chores. When I had enough money saved up, I'd walk two miles to the Darnell Drug Store and buy a balsa wood model airplane kit. My fingers would be cut up from using worn out razor blades to separate the parts from the balsa wood strips. The pieces were put in place with Elmer's Glue and safety pins. When the frame was finished, I covered it with the thin paper sheets that came with the kit and painted it with dope. The models were powered with a rubber band. It was more fun to build them than to watch them fly for a few seconds.

When I got my driver's license, I'd borrow my mother's car to drive to the airport, park outside the fence, and watch the airplanes take off and land. It fascinated me. My high school was on the campus of Notre Dame, which had a wonderful bookstore. One day I bought a book called *The Theory of Wing Sections*. It contained the results of hundreds of wind tunnel tests conducted by the NACA, the predecessor of NASA. The front part of the book contained the mathematical theory of airfoil sections. An airfoil is the cross section of a wing, and is responsible for the lifting capability of the airplane, and the drag of the wing. While I was okay in math, the formulas didn't interest me much. What did interest me were the results they got by carefully changing the shapes and retesting them. If you were designing an airplane in those days, you'd go to this book and pick out an airfoil suitable for your design. The coordinates that defined the shapes were printed in the book. I wondered if there was an easier way than building a model and testing it in a wind tunnel. Wouldn't it be great if you could put those coordinates into a computer and have it predict the behavior instead of building it and testing it?

From the time I started high school, I always had a summer job. After my freshman year in college, I started taking flying lessons. It took a few day's wages to pay for a single hour of instruction. The airplane rented for $15.00 per hour, and the instructor added another $10.00. I always ran out of money and had to wait until the following year to resume my training. Meanwhile, I studied for my Private Pilot written examination and passed the test easily. I finally got my license after graduation from college. The first passenger I took for a ride was my sister, Diane, who was not so sure that she liked it.

After I got my first job, I saved up enough money for a down payment on my own airplane. I put down a deposit on a Cessna 177 located in Pennsylvania, but never got the airplane—or my money back. I went there to confront the "dealer," who turned out to have a grass strip on his farm. The airplane was part of a deal he was putting together that fell apart. He never got the airplane, was out of business, and had no money. Suing him would have cost more than I could recover, so I was basically screwed.

I found another airplane that looked promising, a Rockwell 112A located in Oklahoma. This time I checked the dealer out thoroughly. Since I did not have an endorsement to fly an airplane with retractable gear and a constant speed propeller, I took my flight instructor John Miller with me to fly the airplane home. While it was mechanically sound, the doors didn't fit right and there were other problems with it. Still, I was now an airplane owner.

One of the flight instructors at the South Bend airport was a young lady who actually lived in Columbus, Ohio. She had her own airplane too. I talked to her about my interest in airfoils and aeronautical theory, and she suggested that I fly down to Columbus for a weekend with her, and she would take me to the Aeronautical & Astronautical Research Laboratory. I think she had the ulterior motive of seeing if I was boyfriend material. So I went. At the lab I met Dr. Gerald Gregorek, who had received a contract from NASA to develop new airfoil sections using a computer program written by a German Professor named Richard Eppler. Dr. G, as everyone calls him, spent a lot of time talking to me. He was surprised that a non-engineering graduate knew so much about airfoil theory and airfoils. He volunteered to drive me to a local used bookstore and pick out a couple of books that he thought I should study. He offered to answer any questions I had as I went through them and gave me his phone number.

The difference between learning on your own and taking a formal course is that you can go slowly. I didn't want to just learn a bunch of equations; I wanted to know what those equations meant. For example, when I got to the part discussing something called induced drag, I couldn't really understand how they came up with their formula. The theory originated with Max Munk. I went to the Notre Dame engineering library and checked out both of his books. I went through his discovery carefully, retracing the path that he took, and came out totally understanding what was going on. I did that with a lot of other concepts too. While the textbooks gave me the bottom line, they skimped on how to get to the conclusion. The other problem is that mathematicians like to reduce equations to their smallest possible form. That almost always hides the physical processes underlying them. For example, you find terms like "pounds times seconds squared over feet to the fourth power." What on earth is a square second? Working it backwards, I learned where that came from. I think students in a formal course are given so many new things all at once that they barely have time to memorize a bunch of formulas much less time to really understand them. I have a passion for understanding the underlying physics in every equation.

Many years ago, there was a company in nearby Benton Harbor called Heath. They packaged and sold various electronic items in kit form. You would get a printed circuit board, a pile of resistors, capacitors, and instructions that guided you through the construction process. You had to solder all the pieces together yourself. The Heathkits came with a nice cabinet or box so that you would have a good looking finished product. I built several complex things, like a color television, a microwave, and the alarm clock that still works after forty years.

Long before the age of Radio Shack TRS-80s, or Apples, or IBM PC's, Heath made a kit using the new Intel 8080 Microprocessor, called the H-8. I had to have one. It was basically a box with an LED digital display and a bunch of buttons on the front. You could attach a cassette tape recorder to it to store your programs. Very little software was available at that time for the new microprocessors. Then Heath came out with a monitor for it, called the H-9. It was a television tube, and the keyboard was made up of individual buttons each of which had to be separately installed and soldered together. It was really crude, but it worked. Next came a floppy disk drive. That was a huge improvement over tape cassettes. Memory for the H-8 was really expensive. I think I spent $450 for three printed circuit boards, each containing only 8,000 bytes of memory. So I had a total of 24,000 bytes (24K) of memory. In contrast, the computer I'm using right now came with 8 GB (8 trillion) bytes of memory as standard equipment.

The world of home computers at that time consisted of hobbyists.

The internet didn't exist. The computer at Notre Dame, a Univac 1107, took up a whole room and required a team of people to keep it running. The idea of a small computer seemed like a joke. Among the hobbyists, the challenge was to increase the amount of software available, by taking programs written for the big machines and adapting them to run on our little machines.

I had started my programming experience using Assembly Language. Computers are really dumb. They can only move things around, add or subtract. Assembly Language was a way to tell the computer what to do. A typical instruction might be MOV A,C. That would take the contents of register A and move it to register C. If you wanted to multiply or divide, it might take hundreds of commands to find the answer, because it could only add or subtract. But through this process I truly understood how digital technology works.

When Intel came out with the 8085, an upgraded and faster version of the 8080, I decided to build a new computer from scratch. I ordered a motherboard from one company, a power supply from another, two eight-inch floppy drives from Siemens, and wired it all together on a piece of ½-inch thick particle board. I named it HAL, after the computer in *2001: A Space Odyssey*. The best operating system was called CP/M. It contained all the software needed to read, write, and keep track of files. However, it was hardware independent, so to make it work you had to write your own routines to talk to your specific hardware.

This was fun. I learned to think like a machine. Most of the time the computer is waiting for you to do something. It constantly checks the keyboard. The process goes "get the status byte from the keyboard. Check to see if a character was typed. If not, repeat. When the status shows that a key was pressed, get the character from the keyboard. Tell the keyboard we have the letter. Reset the status byte." A disk drive was more complicated. There was a hole punched in the 8-inch floppy disk. You had to wait until a light shined through the hole, which let you know where you were on the disk. You had to move the recording/reading head to the right place, then wait a given number of microseconds so that the head stopped shaking. I learned a lot about hardware by writing the interface for my homebuilt computer.

Finally, a New York company called Lifeboat Associates came out with a FORTRAN compiler for microprocessors. This was something I had waited for. I had ordered a copy of Richard Eppler's computer program, which Ohio State was using to design airfoils. I typed that program into the computer one letter at a time. It was very long and took days. In the process I learned the FORTRAN programming language. I also found some errors. I notified NASA whenever I found one.

Since there was no way I could run the program with only 24K of memory, I decided to break the program into modules and run one module at a time. I wrote an Assembly Language program to handle the chore of saving the variables, reading the ones it needed for the next step, and loading another module. It was not easy. But it worked! I could run the sample cases in the report and get identical results. While the big mainframes might take a minute, my homebuilt computer might take an hour, but we got the same answers.

I began typing in the coordinates from the *Theory of Wing Sections* and compared my answers to their test results. Not perfect, but close. I also experimented with designing new airfoil sections of my own and testing them. By making hundreds of changes, I formed a mental picture of how things worked.

Burt Rutan was an engineer in California who had started a company selling plans for an airplane called VariViggen that you could build at home. It was made of wood, like the model airplanes Burt designed and flew as radio controlled models, and won many trophies. I bought a set of plans at the EAA convention in Oshkosh, which is the largest air show in the world. Burt then designed a new airplane. To save time he made patterns, glued them to a block of Styrofoam, and used a heated wire to cut out the shape of the wing. It worked! The foam would then be covered with fiberglass. It was strong and light, and permitted him to get the plane built very quickly. He named the plane Vari-Eze. He brought the first one to Oshkosh, and it created a sensation. I bought a set of plans for that also.

The wing sections were drawn full size in the plans, but there were no coordinates given. I took a digital micrometer and a magnifying glass, and carefully measured many points on the drawing, creating my own set of coordinates. I put these into my computer and analyzed them.

Burt was working on a new design, a self-launching sailplane. It would have a motor and propeller on a retractable arm, so that a person could launch their glider without hiring a tow plane. Once aloft the arm could be retracted, forming a streamlined shape. He went to NASA for help in selecting airfoil sections, but NASA did not have data for the speed and lift he needed. Someone suggested that there was a guy in Indiana who might be able to help. Burt called me and then sent coordinates for some airfoils he was considering. I was happy to type them in and run analyses on them. I had a printer, but no way to plot results, so I did that by hand. For the heck of it I threw in a couple of my own designs that I thought had better results. I made a cassette recording walking him through the printouts and plots.

To make a long story short, Burt ended up using my airfoils on the Solitaire self-launching sailplane. It worked well. We were both intrigued with the fact that instead of picking wing sections out of a book, they could be custom tailored for each individual airplane. My next assignment was Voyager, which would become the first airplane in history to circumnavigate the earth on a single tank of gas. It now hangs in the Smithsonian's National Air & Space Museum. I also designed its propellers. Whenever Burt was designing a new airplane, I'd develop new airfoil sections optimized for it.

I had also taken another NASA computer program, called a vortex-lattice method, and modified it to give me the information that an airplane designer needed, like how much lift each section of the wing was producing, and whether the airplane was stable. Burt was using Apple computers, and I built CP/M cards for them so that I could run my FORTRAN programs on them. I continued to use my homebuilt one.

It amazes me how we did so much with so little. We didn't even have a modem. I would call Burt's secretary and read hundreds of seven-digit numbers over the phone, which would then be used to generate plots on their large HP plotter.

Burt's airplanes attracted a lot of attention. After the launch of Voyager, I came home to find two television trucks parked in my driveway. I started giving technical papers describing the design details at SAE (Society of Automotive Engineers) and AIAA (American Institute of Aeronautics and Astronautics) conventions. Jack Cox wrote a feature article about me in *Sport Aviation*. Meanwhile Burt kept cranking out airplanes, and I was busy trying to keep up with him.

The biggest project he did was for Beech Aircraft. Gas prices had doubled, consequently the days of running around in private jets, which are fuel hogs, seemed numbered. Beech wanted something with the interior size of a private jet, with the operating economy of a turboprop. Burt came up with two possibilities, and I did the stability calculations for them. Beech favored a design that resembled the VariEze or its larger brother, the Long-EZ. It was a very complicated design. I created something called a blended wing, with five separate airfoil sections blended into one piece, so that each part of the wing had its own optimized shape, but operated as one whole. The forward wing was swept back for cruising flight and made straight for takeoff or landing. I did the stability calculations for the airplane with flaps up and down, forward wing swept and unswept. It took most of my time for several months.

Since I had done so much work on it, Beech offered me a contract to help support them through the process of FAA certification. I agreed. This was my baby too, and I wanted it to be successful.

I also managed to get permission from Beech to take some time to design a radical wing-sail for the first catamaran ever used in the America's Cup race. We won. I also designed my first airplane from a clean sheet of paper, the Eagle X-TS, produced in Australia. I was honored in London at a gala awards banquet for that design, receiving the Grand Master's Medal. The Grand Master is His Royal Highness Prince Philip. *Air & Space* magazine, published by the Smithsonian, did a feature article about me. The AIAA named me a Distinguished Lecturer, and I went around the country giving a presentation on the planes I had worked on, and what the challenges were. I was named an "Old Master" by Purdue University, and went there to teach some classes, and to meet with aero engineering students in the evenings to give them an opportunity to ask questions. I guest lectured at seven other universities. I have received so many awards that they fill a whole wall.

I have given many talks over the years at the annual EAA Convention in Oshkosh, teaching theory. I became very concerned that some of the kits being offered were dangerous. They were unstable in pitch. I decided to write a series of articles for *Sport Aviation*. Published over a twelve-month period, I invented spreadsheets that readers could copy, giving them the tools they needed to calculate stability, trim, and all the other data they'd need to determine whether their proposed designs would work and be safe. As a result, both of the unsafe airplane kits were modified to make them stable. Although I never got a penny for all that work, I'm proud to think I have saved a few lives by doing it.

As I write this, I've done work on fifty-three designs. I've written hundreds of programs to help in this work. I'm busy on number fifty-four now. Years of experience and testing, and having the custom software tools makes it relatively simple to nail down a design. I do still get challenges. I took on the task of doing the detail aerodynamic design of GlobalFlyer, in which Steve Fossett became the first person to fly solo around the world on a single tank of gas. That airplane is also in the Smithsonian now. It was a huge challenge, and it succeeded. I'm very proud of the fact that it not only circumnavigated the earth, but the performance was so amazing that in an attempt to set another world record, he flew around the world again, and continued all the way to England afterwards on the original tank of gas! The extra range is due to the hard work I did in optimizing it.

I finally had a chance to repay a debt. PADA (The Personal Aircraft Design Academy) gave me their prestigious award at a banquet during the EAA Convention. In my acceptance speech, I started by telling the story of how I met Dr. Gregorek, how he took me to a bookstore and selected books for me, and how he helped me by answering a slew of questions over the years. I was not his student. I didn't even go to his school. This was something that few people would ever do for someone else. I held up the trophy, looked at him in the audience, and with a voice cracking with emotion, said simply, "Dr. G, this is for you." The whole room broke into applause.

About the Author

JOHN RONCZ BEGAN his aeronautical career by building a computer and then adapting a NASA airfoil analysis code to run on it. He spent months learning airfoil theory and comparing computer predictions to wind tunnel tests. When Burt Rutan heard of his work, he asked John to analyze some airfoil candidates for his Solitaire sailplane. John sent him the results for these along with some of his own airfoil designs for comparison. Burt chose the Roncz airfoil section, which worked very well. This led to a collaboration that lasted over twenty years, in which time Burt developed configurations and John analyzed the stability and designed custom airfoil sections for each airplane.

John is responsible for some portion of more than fifty aircraft designs. The most recent to fly is the Icon A5, an amphibious Light Sport Aircraft. He was responsible for the aerodynamic design and performance of the GlobalFlyer, a radical jet in which Steve Fossett recently set three world records. It was the second airplane John worked on that was placed in the National Air & Space Museum. He has designed sixteen propellers and wind turbines, including the propellers for the globe-circling Voyager and the prototype Starship. Venturing outside the aircraft field,

he designed the radical wing-sailed catamaran, which successfully defended the America's Cup in 1988, and a winning WSC
class race car. John was profiled in *Air & Space* magazine, published by the Smithsonian. He wrote twelve articles for *Sport Avi-*
ation and has guest lectured at eight Universities, including being
honored as an "Old Master" by Purdue University. Among his
awards are the Stanley Dzik memorial trophy, the Honor Roll of
Professional Pilot magazine, the Medal of Achievement from *Sail-*
ing World magazine, the Professor August Raspet award, and the
Milwaukee School of Engineering Gold Medal. John served as a
"Distinguished Lecturer" for the American Institute of Aeronautics and Astronautics. In November 2000 he was honored by His
Royal Highness Prince Philip at a ceremony in London, where he
was presented with the Prince's Australian Medal for the design
of the Eagle.

John is an honors graduate of the University of Notre Dame, an
artist, and a classical pianist. He holds a commercial pilot's license
with multi-engine, instrument and glider ratings and has logged
more than 1800 hours.

13855325R00104

Made in the USA
Charleston, SC
05 August 2012